What Others are Saying About
Always Ready

"Like a conversation studded with sea stories, White's collection ranges from the serious—fractured marriages, war casualties—to the serious silliness of the 360-degree club and Golden Dragon initiation."

—Jacquelyn Bengfort, U.S. Navy veteran
and author of *Navy News Service*
and *Suitable for All Methods of Communication*

"White's poetry serves as a magnifying glass that enhances the details and allows them to tell the whole story. The direct style throughout *Always Ready* is as mesmerizing as it is powerful. White's presentation of his career is raw and full of keen observations, humor, mischief, and tragedy. There is a chapter's worth of insight on every page! I never thought that so few words could hit me so hard. White seems to have truly seen it all!"

—Caroline Walsh, U.S. Coast Guard veteran
and author of *Fairly Smooth Operator:*
My Life Occasionally at the Tip of the Spear

"Veterans and military families of all eras and branches will delight in White's sharp humor and storytelling. His stories of adventures and misadventures are sure to variously inspire laughter, reflection, and patriotic pride!"

—Randy Brown, U.S. Army veteran and author of
Welcome to FOB Haiku:
War Poetry from Inside the Wire

"There are libraries full of books on Navy, Army, Air Force, and Marine Corps topics, but fewer on the U.S. Coast Guard. *Always Ready* cures that by delivering a huge spectrum of observations—everything from the deck plates to the engine rooms. It's at times funny, at times poignant, and always deeply revelatory of the Coast Guard experience few know and fewer understand. Strongly recommended!"

—Daniel Charles Ross,
U.S. Navy veteran
and author of *Force No One: A Thriller*

"Benjamin White's poems—sharp, pithy, at times hilarious and at times gutting—showcase the beautiful and bizarre moments in the country's least-known military service. *Always Ready* is a captivating tour of White's time in the Coast Guard, and his poems illuminate the genuine humanity of a life spent in uniform."

—Sonner Kehrt,
U.S. Coast Guard veteran
and investigative reporter for *The War Horse Journal*

"Among the beauties of White's energetic paean to the Coast Guard are some striking poems about military families. From 'The Family Pants,' for example: 'But worse than that / He would have to face his wife, / A classmate of his from the Academy / Who gave up her own career ...' A great read that contains surprises!"

—Frederick Foote, U.S. Navy veteran
and author of *Medic Against Bomb:
A Doctor's Poetry of War*

Always Ready

Poems from a Life
in the U.S. Coast Guard

Benjamin B. White
Middle West Press LLC
Johnston, Iowa

Poetry / Military Life / Humor & Memoir

*Always Ready:
Poems from a Life in the U.S. Coast Guard*
by Benjamin B. White

ISBN (print): 978-1-953665-08-9
ISBN (e-book): 978-1-953665-09-6
Library of Congress Control Number: 2022941655

Middle West Press LLC
P.O. Box 1153
Johnston, Iowa 50131-9420
www.middlewestpress.com

*Special thanks to James Burns of Denver, Colorado!
Your patronage helps publish great military-themed writing!*
www.aimingcircle.com

*This book is dedicated
to all the stories the Coast Guard
can and can't remember,
the people who told and tell them,
and the servicemembers who lived and live them*

CONTENTS

Poems from a Life in the U.S. Coast Guard

NOTES ON POEMS

A FEW WORDS OF THANKS

ABOUT THE WRITER

DID YOU ENJOY THIS BOOK?

When Jaws Drop

It's the professional mindset
Of commercial fishermen
That instead of calling
The Coast Guard for assistance
                    They'd rather
Go back to port
And get a bigger boat—

But they will get eaten by sharks
Before they ever do that.

Always Ready

If a person says, "Semper Fidelis"
You immediately think of
The United State Marine Corps,

But if someone says, "Semper Paratus"
It's easy to think it sounds
Like some kind of fish, or maybe a disease.
And around the world
On seven seas, the Coast Guard
Knows what it means:

"Always Ready."

The fifth military branch
Holding steady since 1790
With a tiny force about as big
As the New York City Police Department.
With missions promoting visions of success
From aids to navigation, law enforcement,
Search-and-rescue, icebreaking,
Wiping oil off rocks and ducks,
Eating snakes in Colombia,
Delivering humanitarian aid,
And regulating the catch of international
Fisheries in the Bering Sea—

"Being all we can be" in our own right—

All the snazzy Latin
Semper Paratus

Got us no recognition—
Never did anything
For the identity crisis
Or the chip
On our organizational shoulder.

So, here's a tip:

Don't even mention
The Navy
To a Coast Guardsman.

BENJAMIN B. WHITE

The Navy

The Navy has always been too big
For its own good—
                    Manpower spoiled
                    By manpower—
Going to sea
With 5,000 sailors onboard,
Having too many Admirals
On the policy board
And changing uniforms
Every six months.
Recruiting pilots
To fly jets
In a sea-going service—
                    And training;
                    Always training—
The Navy is the only organization
That has to cram-jam
Two days of training
Into a week
Just to accommodate
All the necessary smoke breaks.

Ski Boat

I worked for a guy
I would work for
Anytime, anywhere ...
                    And he told me
It was possible
To ski behind
A 44-foot Motor Lifeboat
                        Though he stopped short
Before telling me
How he knew that.

Alligator

The coxswain—
Patrolling on the 41-footer
Down in the bayou one night—
Said a state law-enforcement boat
Came up on him
                                    With its blue light on,
So—law enforcement to law enforcement—
He turned his blue light on, too
Just to let the state guy know
                                    He was legit—
And they passed each other
With a professional, blue-tinted wave

And it was a good thing,
The coxswain said,
"Because I had an alligator
Poached in the well deck."

Leadership

Competent leadership
In many forms and flavors
Was so common

When a new Commander
Took over a Group

It was a simple
Yes or no answer
For the crew to know

Within a day or two ...

And when the Commander
Didn't have it,
It was plain to see

And that was enough
To make the crew worry

While hoping
The best of the organization
Would pull
The unit through ...

Most times, it did.

Organizational Structure

The E-2 Seaman—
A brand-new boot right out of Cape May—
Was so proud to be
Part of the Coast Guard
That on watch early one morning
He decided to send an e-mail
                    To the Commandant
                    (Signal number No. 1)—
It was a "Dear Admiral" e-mail
Full of excitement and happiness
Wondering what he should do
To ensure his motivation
Stayed intact
For a whole 30-year career—
                    He hit send;
                    And the Admiral received,
The lines of communication—
Though not the intended lines of communication—
Worked, and worked well
As they flattened
                    The military structure
                    Of the Coast Guard.

The Commandant
Reformed the vertical nature of the service
By simply replying
                    Telling the Seaman
It was good to hear
Such energy and excitement
From the field

While letting the young man know
It was probably better
For him to have
That career-minded discussion
With the Chief at the station—

And *that* discussion
Most likely
Put the higher
Back in hierarchy.

The Family Pants

He would have rather stayed at work
Than go home
Where he would have to face
    His kids
From whom he got no appreciation
And over whom he had no control,
    But worse than that
He would have had to face his wife—
A classmate of his from the Academy
Who gave up her own career
Sacrificing her own aspirations
    To raise his family—
A duty assignment
She hated,
And hated him for,
    So if he had any complaints
About his job,
The crew,
Or his Executive Officer,
    She would naturally
Slip into her military bearing
And tell him
He was handling the whole situation
Of his command wrong,
    Until one day,
He relieved his XO,
Alienated the crew,
Couldn't define job satisfaction,
And still dreaded going home.

Faithful

Everybody at the unit knew—
Well, everybody
But her husband knew—
She was having an affair
               So when he
               Inevitably found out,
He actually felt
Just as betrayed,
If not more so,
By the silence
Of his secretive shipmates
               Than he felt
               About her infidelity ...

That was career-minded
And professionally loyal,
But probably demonstrated
His dedication to the organization
               That led her
               To being unfaithful
               In the first place.

Legend

He was a rescue swimmer
And the signal for him to jump
Out of the helicopter
                    Was a pat on the shoulder,
But the Public Affairs Specialist
Was trying to get pictures
Of the city skyline
And patted him on the shoulder
                    Just to get him
                    To scoot over—
All he felt
Was the signal to go,
So he went —
Jumping out
And down
Into the muddy shoreline
                    Where he broke
                    Both his legs ...

He'd be the first to laugh
If you told him
He didn't have a leg to stand on—
                    And that's the stuff
                    Coast Guard legends
                    Are made of.

Cocaine

The Group Commander listened
As the Second Class Petty Officer
Explained how she was
A terrible judge of character,
Had gotten in with the wrong people,
And had, in fact, indulged

                In cocaine use—
With her career on the line
Her performance
And excellent boat-driving skills
Were mixed-in
To the decision,

                And despite
                The Deputy Group Commander
                Advising against it,
The Group Commander deviated
From all organizational norms,
Applied confidence in his leadership skills,
And gave her a second chance
To demonstrate she had learned a lesson ...

                She wasn't discharged—
Well, at least not until
She popped positive
On her next urinalysis

                Giving the command
                No choice
                But to kick her out.

Deal

I was about to graduate college
And get married,
So I was looking
For a future

            When I went back
            To the Army

And asked
If they'd send me
To OCS—

            The recruiter said, "Yes!
            We'd love to have you back!"

Then I asked him
What MOS he could offer,
And he said,

            "You were Infantry before,
            You'll be Infantry again."

Suddenly, the Coast Guard
Looked like
A pretty good deal.

Indoctrination

Army OCS would have been 17 weeks—
                    Which wasn't really appealing
                    To a newlywed—
But the Coast Guard recruiter said
If I enlisted,
I could join,
And attend 3.5 weeks
Of Prior Service Indoctrination Training
                    At Cape May, New Jersey.
Paraphrasing the Army recruiter,
I had been enlisted before
I could be enlisted again,
                    So I took the oath,
And shipped out
For initial training
With a group of people
                    Who had seen the light
Coming in from DoD services ...

We gathered at the Training Center
For what turned out to be
A requirement to
                    Learn the ranks and rates,
                    Sit through some training videos,
                    Get a sea bag full of uniforms,
And watch a lot of MTV.

Swim

I didn't know how to swim
But to graduate
From my initial training program,
I had to complete a lap
In the big Olympic-sized pool,
                So I pulled myself
Down and back
With a breast stroke
And frantic kicking
              Then I celebrated
          Not drowning
By never looking back,
Philosophically and pragmatically convinced
If I ever needed to swim,
In the line of duty
                Something had gone
                Terribly wrong.

Identity

There was always the identity problem
As the fifth military branch
Tucked into
The Department of Treasury
Then the Department of Transportation,
Then later moved as plank-owners
In the Department of Homeland Security.

So, lesson No. 1
For every member
Was the truth—

                    The Coast Guard is
The hard core
About which
The Navy forms
In times of war.

Shut Up

It was an issue of culture
And Coast Guard people with no prior service
In another military branch
                    Hated to hear
Their shipmates who had joined
The Coast Guard as a second choice
                    Start off any discussion—

A solution,
An idea,
Or even just a story—

With, "Well, in the [insert DoD service here]
We used to [fill in the blank]

Those discussions were quickly met
With, "This isn't the [insert DoD service here],"
And more frequently
With a quick and strict
                    "Shut up."

Stress

Getting underway
Always put stress
                        On families—
Still, no one thought seriously twice
About it when the shipped pulled in,
The cook got a ride home, and
                        Before going inside,
She said, "I hope he doesn't kill me."

                        By her next duty day,
The crew knew
Her husband
Had shot her
Shortly after
She'd walked
Through the door.

Initiation

Before the Golden Dragons
Could become Golden Dragons
They were blindfolded
                    And taken through
The passages into the ancient realm
Where they would receive
King Neptune's favor
By kissing his hairy, fat stomach,
Then swim through
The Whale's Belly
Where a month's worth
Of throwaway food scraps
Had been mixed and kept
                    For effect,
And the last act,
Before being accepted
Was to strip off
All the nasty clothes
That had served as a uniform
During the initiation,
And throw them in the ocean—
                    Thus ending
A week full
Of all the evils
Shipmates could think of ...

Although a Chief Storekeeper
Did have to intervene
To prevent the chemicals
Of the deodorizing urinal cakes

From being rubbed
On the faces
Of the soon-to-be initiated.

Sextant

The requirement was to use a sextant
And get a reading of a heading
Within so many degrees—
                              So the Officer Candidate
Went through the prescribed steps,
Called out the heading,
And hid his surprise
When it was checked off
                              As correct.

Proudly relieved
To be sextant-qualified,
He subsequently
Put the instrument down
And walked away
Never to apply
                              The skill
                              Ever again

Gig Line

It was Coast Guard Indoctrination at its best—

The explanation of the gig line:
>   The edge of the shirt
>   Lined up with the belt buckle
>   Lined up with the trousers' fly.
Top-notch training
For a group with an average
Of nine years of service—

Even the prior Air Force guy
>   Let his sarcasm show:

"You would have had
To have been in the military
To know that."

BENJAMIN B. WHITE

Dress Pants

The Tropical Blue Long uniform
Required blue polyester pants,
But there were never enough
In the right size available
Through the Coast Guard Exchange
                              Supply lines,
                              But the organization
Was built on a reputation
Of finding solutions
And the Air Force pants
Were the same color
                    And polyester was polyester

Although if you looked closely,
You would notice the USAF polyester
Was a different blend,
A different material,
So wearing them
Was not authorized—

                    Until necessity
                    (and unauthorized practice)
                    Changed policy.

Point No-Point

It was a unit-level morale opportunity,
To stay the night in the lighthouse—
                    Isolated
With the ghosts of the ocean
Clinging to tradition and lore ...

                    The Coast Guard had changed
Along with missions,
Technology, navigation,
And even society,
                    But a night
At the lighthouse
Would remind you
Of all the right
And romantic reasons
                    For which
                    You had joined the service

Spare Parts

There was a Commander renting a house
From a Lieutenant stationed
                              On the East Coast
Who had every intention of getting back
To Seattle for his next tour—
                              But someone
Told the Lieutenant
That the Commander,
                              A mechanic,
                              Constant machinist,
                              And mechanical innovator
Had cluttered the yard
On pristine Bainbridge Island
With all kinds of engine parts—
                              From appliances,
                              Scooters, cars, and boats,
And the Lieutenant
Was more than a little worried—
But needlessly so
Because the Commander
Would never transfer anywhere
                              Without the entire collection.

Success

The Academy graduates
Go through four—
                    Sometimes five—
Years of being told
How special and elite they are,
                    Then they graduate
Into their commitment,
Buy their first cars,
And get welcomed
                    Into the realm
Of real expectations
That enlisted people
Must meet for them
So those officers can have
                    Successful careers.

Rank Has Its Medals

The Meritorious Service Medal
Was an O-5 citation—
                          Anyone below Commander
Only rated a Coast Guard Commendation
                          (Or less)
No matter what
They had done
Or how they had performed.

Heroes

The Coast Guard's one recipient
Of the Medal of Honor
Is cherished, idolized, memorialized—
                                    With cutters,
Buildings, and every station mascot dog
Named Munro—
And rightfully so,
As he extracted Marines
From Guadalcanal
Saving their lives despite
                                    Deadly wounds of his own—
But on D-Day,
Dedicated coxswains
Took the Infantry in
With just as much—
                                    If not more—
Suppressive fire against them
And their Higgins Crafts—
                                    And flying helicopters
Into hurricanes
Is an honorable feat—
                                    And pulling people
Out of rough seas
Takes no small amount
Of bravery—
                                    And saving people
From nowhere-to-go
Boat fires
Is pretty heroic—
                                    And patrolling jungles

Along Vietnam rivers
And again in Colombia
Took a special kind of devotion—
                              And getting people
Away from the deadly suction
Of a sinking vessel
Is courageous—
                              But above all these feats,
Maintaining a tradition held dear
By all the members of an organization
Is also a matter of duty,
So in a service
Full of heroes, one hero
Is enough.

360

There wasn't much age difference
Between the junior enlisted
And the junior officers,
                              But the range
Of responsibility was immense,
So it wasn't easy
To distract the officer
With the deck and the conn
Who was navigating the night orders
                              During the midwatch—
Because with varying degrees of stress
They focused on their task
And rarely lost attention
To the compass
And the heading,
                              But sometimes ...
                              Sometimes ...
A young helmsman
Could bring the ship around,
Off course,
Way off course
90-degrees
180-degrees
270-degrees
Then around again
Easing the compass
Back on course
                              Without the officer
Seeing it
Feeling it
Or noticing it at all—

BENJAMIN B. WHITE

                    The 360-degree club
Was an elite group,
And a secret society
Held in great esteem

                    By watchstanders everywhere.

Ring-Knockers

The Coast Guard Academy
Turned out brand-new Ensigns
From its protected hallways
                And its cookie-cutter mold—
All of them holding
The same academic concept of success,
The same ideas of duty,
The same philosophies of leadership,
The same arrogance,
                And the same amount
                Of the shared doubt
                Hidden under false confidence,
And the organization
Was just an extension
Of the life they'd accepted
Right after high school
                As they brought
Their college days to work
Every day for years and careers
Knowing everyone
                From seven graduating classes—
                The three ahead
                And the three behind
                Their own
Moving through the stages
All the same flavor
Wearing their school pride
On their fingers
Ready to demonstrate
New London attitudes
With the expected privileges
                Of ring-knocker camaraderie.

Glory Days

As a seaman
And a Third Class Petty Officer,
I had a college degree—
                    I just didn't have a commission,
So when the young Ensigns
Started talking about
The Academy glory days
Of sports and competition,
                    I would let them know
I played my college baseball
At a Division I school—
                    And the junior officer
From the University of Miami
Would give me
A supportive,
Appreciative smile.

Prior Enlisted

Officers didn't get
Good Conduct citations
Unless they had earned
                    The recognition
While they were enlisted—
In which case,
They could still wear it
After being commissioned ...

                    A Lieutenant Commander
Told me the greatest compliment
He had ever gotten
When he was a Commanding Officer
                    Of a cutter
Was when his crew
Asked him why
He didn't wear
                    His Good Conduct Ribbon.

Spouse

It was really kind of sad
When a senior officer retired,
And then, six months later,
                    The officer—
Lost and without purpose—
Would simply die
With nothing to live for,
                    But it was easy to tell
Which officers were headed
For that fate
Because they wore
Their Academy class ring
On the same finger
                    As their wedding bands
Reminding themselves
And everyone around them
They were married
To the Coast Guard,
                    And like so many
                    People before them,
They were forsaken
By any motivation
To live on
After losing a spouse ...

And their actual wedding bands
Were reminders
That made it all
That much sadder.

Curse

The crew said,
                    The unit was cursed,
And when the new XO arrived,
He could feel the low-morale,
Sad-emotion, black-cloud environment,
And made it his purpose
                    To lift the spirits,
And he did—
For the next two years
                    The crew
Loved coming to work,
Loved their jobs,
Loved the Coast Guard,
Loved their unit—
                    Then the XO was relieved for cause—
The cause being
He paid too much attention
To the people-first initiatives
And the physical-mental well-being
                    Of the crew,
And as he packed up his office,
He had to wonder
If maybe
                    There really was a curse ...

Then he went home
And watched
"Mister Roberts."

37

BENJAMIN B. WHITE

The Coast Guard Song

On those rare occasions
When we could get the tune right—
           After a change of command,
           Some patriotic celebration,
           Or maybe a parade—
It would encourage us to sing along—
           "*Semper Paratus* is our guide,
           Our ba-ba-ba-bah-too
           Do-do-do-do-DO-do-do-do
           Do-do-do-do-doo-doooo"—
But that's all we knew.

Flood

When the MORGENTHAU
Went under the Golden Gate Bridge
And took a starboard turn
Towards Alaska
And cold weather,

           The fuel tanks
           Would sweat and cause

Moisture to collect,
Pools of water to gather,
And a flood to deepen

           In Deckie Berthing

Where anything left on deck
Would be washed away
On the foot-deep ocean

           Gently rocking
           Inside the ship ...

It was a design flaw
That made the Deck Department personnel
And anyone who could hear them complain

           Long for a port turn
           Towards San Diego

BENJAMIN B. WHITE

Hamilton

On August 4, 1990,
The Coast Guard celebrated
Its 200th birthday,
                    And I was stationed
At Training Center Cape May
Where the Exchange sold
Shirts and shorts,
Magnets, key rings,
And a wide assortment
Of commemorative trinkets
While the crew
Reviewed the actions
Of Alexander Hamilton
Long before the musical.

San Diego Breakfast

It was a great breakfast—
        French toast
        And sausage—
And then I turned to
        Ship's work
Painting below decks
Up in the fo'c'sle
Where we were anchored
Just off San Diego
On a beautiful day
        With a gentle rocking
Sway and rhythm,
And we opened the hatch
To let the sunshine find us
And to let in some
Cooler, fresher air,
But that didn't do any good
As the fumes,
The rocking,
The French toast
And sausage grease
        Finally forced me
To put my brush down
And hurry back
To the head
And say goodbye
        To that delicious breakfast.

Speaking Army

Officer Candidate School
Was in Yorktown, Virginia,
And in the later weeks
Of the 17-week program,
        We got our evenings free,
So a classmate and I
Were in the gym one night
Talking to an Army guy.
And my classmate asked him
        What he did
        And he replied,
Saying something about
"Useless and Trepidation"—
        Later, my classmate asked me
What the soldier had said,
And I translated,
"He is at Fort Eustis in Transportation"
And my classmate just shook his head—
        "Man, I'm glad you speak Army.
        I had no idea
        What he said."

Notification

The first Coast Guard war casualty
Since Vietnam
Was a kid from Long Island—
                      Killed by terrorists
                      In the Persian Gulf,
And the District called me
(As the XO of the nearest unit)
To let us know
To start the notifications proceedings,
                      And I briefed it up
To my Commanding Officer,
Asking him
If he wanted me
To go with him and the Chaplain
                      To see and tell the family—

                      I had been the Commanding Officer
                      Of my own unit,
And though this was
An extreme mission
No Coast Guard officer
Had done since the 1970s,
                      I had an understanding
                      Of leadership responsibility
                      And would have dutifully
                      Accompanied him
                      If only for his moral support—
In fact,
I personally thought
I was better suited—

More humanitarian-minded,
More personable,
More sincere,
More genuine

Than the CO—
But he told me no—
Only he would go
With the Chaplain—

When he got back
From delivering the news
To the family,

He was angry at me,
Dressing me down
In front of his desk

For not going,

And telling me
He had needed me there,
And that he had pulled over
To the side of the road

And cried—

Blaming me for not being there
(Making it about himself somehow),
And then telling me he was upset
That flowers hadn't been ordered
From the unit for the family—

And I knew I was right:

I was better suited
To have gone with the Chaplain

And something deep inside me

Froze over
And I lost all respect
For any inkling
Of leadership

He might have had ...

The Senior Chief Yeoman
Heard the one-sided conversation
Through the wall,

       And had flowers delivered
       The next day.

Toll Booth

I was the Commanding Officer
Of the Gulf Region Fisheries Training Center
GRFTC—acronymically pronounced, "GERF-TEC"
We operated out of New Orleans,
But I was on a road trip
In Florida with the instructors
                Teaching Boarding Officers
How to conduct and document
Boardings of fishing vessels
In the Gulf of Mexico—
                One day after training
I was driving us back
To the hotel, and we had to cross
                A bridge with a toll—
The Senior Chief was in the front seat with me
And two Petty Officer Instructors
Were in the back seat,
                And one of them told me
                To tell the toll-taker
We were in the Coast Guard
And then we wouldn't have to pay the toll—
                He said, "Sir,
                Just say 'Coast Guard'"
That made sense,
So I did—
I even said it like the Petty Officer
Had said it, loud and clear; plain and bold,
                "Coast Guard!"
The toll-taker just looked at me,
So I said it again,

"Coast Guard!"
And the toll-taker said,
"Fifty cents or turn around,"
And suddenly I heard
Soft, quiet laughter—
                    A kind of giggle—
Coming from the back seat
And the Senior Chief
Was handing me two quarters
Unable to hide
His own smile—
                    You know ...
                    I loved that crew.

By The Book

I had orders to transfer
And I thanked the Chief
I'd been working for—
                Telling him
I appreciated all I had learned from him
And for all the leadership he had demonstrated ...

              He shook my hand,
              Smiled, and replied,
"Well, I didn't always go
By the book,
But I always did
What was right."

It was a lesson
              I've always remembered.

Filed

He was an YN2
Who would have been a YN1
If he hadn't misappropriated
A government car
On Governor's Island
                    One night along his career,
And he was pragmatic about duty—
If it didn't need to be done,
He wasn't going to do it,
                    So when we'd come in
                    Off a patrol
Any filing of paperwork
Into personnel folders
That he had left to do
                    Would be taped up
                    Into a bundle
With a stapler,
Or a two-hole punch,
Or a paperweight—
                    Anything heavy,
So when he threw
The paperwork overboard
It was guaranteed to sink—

                    There was nothing
That would get
In the way
Of liberty.

BENJAMIN B. WHITE

Organizational Diversity

One day after a lunchtime workout,
A Black Petty Officer
In the locker room asked me,
                              "Sir,
What's your first name?"
And I told him, "Ben."

He said, "Ben. Ben White.
                    Mr. Ben White."
He reflected a little bit,
Smiled, and said,
                              "Sir,
You've got a brother's name."

I've never been sure
What that even meant,
But I just smiled back,
And took it as a compliment.

Recognition

The Commander had been
The Training Officer
At Cape May
When I was a Third Class
Marine Science Technician
              And then one day,
At Coast Guard Headquarters,
She got on the same elevator
I was on—
              I recognized her
Right away,
But it took a minute
For my identity
To register with her—
              We hadn't seen each other
              Since before
              I'd gone to OCS—
But in-between floors,
It came to her,
And she nodded her head,
Looking at my Ensign bars,
              And just before
              Stepping off the elevator
She said,
"Those look good on you."

              And I realized,
The pride I had
For my accomplishment
Was shared
By the organization.

Act of Congress

When I was commissioned,
I accepted the responsibility
                    Suddenly gaining
A different attitude
Towards honor and ethics;
Duty and leadership;
Service and self—
                    And I stepped up
                    With accountability
                    And high expectations,
And it wasn't that I had been
A poor enlisted performer—

It was just that I understood
                    It took Senate approval
To make me
An Officer and a Gentleman.

Uniform Gedunk

On one hand,
I understood and empathized
With the pride
Of personal accomplishments,
               But on the other hand,
The Coast Guard
Had to draw the line
Only allowing
Certain ribbons and medals
From other services
               To be worn on their uniforms
So in the end,
I had to fundamentally agree
No one in the Coast Guard
               Should wear jump wings
               Or a Combat Infantryman Badge.

Intimidation

He intimidated
A lot of junior officers,
And—in fact—
A lot of senior officers
              And if the designated crewmember
Didn't bring him the morning paper,
He would send it back
              Demanding
              Order and discipline,
And when he took over the job
As the 8th District Chief of Staff
He required people
Who commuted in
Wearing mufti
To wear no-less-than
              Business casual—
I equated that to when
George Steinbrenner
Said of the New York Yankees,
              "I pay them
Like young executives,
So they will dress
Like young executives."
              And I admired
What the Captain was doing
And just made sure
I never had a reason
To feel intimidated
              At all.

Appearance Over Action

When he retired,
He took with him

> *Command ashore experience*
> *Command afloat experience*
> *A law degree*
> *High expectations*
> *High standards*
> *A reputation of success*
> *Professionalism*
> *Leadership*, and—

Having not been selected for Admiral—

> *Disappointment*

Frustrated with the performance-based system
That he saw—

> And many saw—

As having failed him ...

When he spoke of that disappointment
At his retirement ceremony,
It didn't take long
For the organization

> To take action

And protect selection-board decisions
That were meant
To change the complexion
Of flag-level officers—

Despite his record,
His career became a victim—
A sacrifice in the necessity

BENJAMIN B. WHITE

For the Coast Guard
To change the appearance of
The organization being
A white man's canoe club.

OERs

The flag level was shocked
To find out
Ensigns and Lieutenants (junior grade)
Were writing their own
Officer Evaluation Reports
Instead of having supervisors
Meeting the responsibility
Of using OERs
As a mentoring
And development tool—
                      The shock
Didn't change anything
As I not only
Filled out my own OER,
But helped another Ensign
                      Write his as well.

On Report

Always late to work,
The young Petty Officer
Had become a leadership challenge,
And his chain-of-command

                    Came to me
                    As the XO,

For a solution ...

I prepared a Page 7—

                    A form used
                    To document performance—

Putting myself
And my lack of leadership
On report
And had it ready

                    For him to sign ...

He read it,
And I took full responsibility
Encouraging him
To document my failure
As his Executive Officer
Unable to get him
To work on time ...

                    He refused to sign it,
                    But was never late again.

National Coast Guard

Upon hearing,
"I'm in the Coast Guard,"
People would routinely reply,
                    "Oh, so,
You only have to report
One weekend a month?"
                    Or else ask,
"Where do you go
For your two weeks
In the summer?"

Cockpit

The lieutenant was applying
For Flight School,
But her Commanding Officer
Wasn't going to endorse
                    Her packet—

"Because," he said,
"They call it
A 'cockpit'
For a reason ..."

                    The last I heard,
She was flying helicopters,
And her CO
Was no longer
In the service.

Warrant Officers

Warrant Officers
Were the foulest,
Least-agreeable,
Most-miserable,
Unhappiest,
And crustiest

        Group of people
On the face of the earth—

        But everyone one of them
Made the Coast Guard
A better place ...

        Usually one retirement
At a time.

Chief's Academy, or ... "A Story to Tell"

The Chief Gunner's Mate
Was one of the funniest people
In the organization, and always
Had a story to tell, so when
We happened to run into each other
At Petaluma, of course, he stopped to talk—

                And I was listening to him,
But I felt a little nervous
When I saw his classmates
In the Chief's Academy waiting
For him to get on the bus
So they could get on their way
And complete the training agenda
For the day ...

                He just laughed
When I pointed out
That they were waiting,
And he said,
           "Oh, it's all right,
I'm not doing too good
In the program, anyway."

              People with stories to tell
              Always left me
              With stories to tell.

NOTES ON POEMS

"Act of Congress": Under the U.S. system, a president nominates a person to receive a commission as a military officer, but it is the legislature that approves the rank. Officers swear to support and defend the Constitution for the indefinite time of the commission. Enlisted members swear similar oaths, but contract for discrete time periods.

"Alligator": A coxswain (pronounced "KAWK-sin") is a job title of someone who is qualified to direct a small boat, along with its attendant crew activities.

"Always Ready": The motto of the U.S. Coast Guard is "Semper Paratus." (In Latin, the phrase means "Always Ready.") The words appear on the official Coast Guard flag. The march of the U.S. Coast Guard, written in 1928, is also titled "Semper Paratus." Reportedly, the phrase can be informally shortened to "Semper P," in a manner similar to colloquially abbreviating the U.S. Marine motto from "Semper Fidelius" ("Always Faithful") to "Semper Fi."

"Commanding Officer": In some administrative proceedings regarding disciplinary offenses, commanders may exercise discretion in whether or not to place a servicemember under punishment or probation.

"Cockpit": The initialism "CO" in this context stands for "Commanding Officer."

"Curse": An Executive Officer (XO) is a captain's nominal second-in-command, and is often the day-to-day manager of an organization's human resources, maintenance, and other critical efforts. In the 1955 movie "Mister Roberts," starring Henry Fonda and James Cagney, a combat-hungry junior officer of a World War II U.S. Navy cargo ship engages a tyrannical commanding officer in a battle of wills, on behalf of a suffering crew.

"Deal": In the U.S. Army and Marine Corps, jobs are abbreviated and described by a system of alphanumeric codes called Military Occupational Specialties (M.O.S.). For example, a U.S. Army Infantry soldier holds an MOS of 11-B ("11-Bravo"), while a soldier trained as a mortarman holds an MOS of 11-C ("11-Charlie"). In the U.S. Coast Guard and Navy, jobs are described by a system of "ratings."

After attending a 17-week Officer Candidate School (O.C.S.) course of instruction, during which they are trained in leadership, management, navigation, law enforcement, and other military subjects, enlisted members receive a commission as an officer in the U.S. Coast Guard. They begin at a rank of "Ensign."

"Dress Pants": Servicemembers must maintain a variety of duty and dress uniforms, of which the wear and appearance of each is prescribed by regulation. The "Exchange" refers the military equivalent of a department store, where servicemembers can often purchase uniform clothing items and insignia at their own expense. The initialism "USAF" refers to the U.S. Air Force.

"The Family Pants": An Executive Officer (XO) is a captain's nominal second-in-command, and is often the day-to-day manager of an organization's human resources, maintenance, and other critical efforts.

"Filed": A yeoman is a Coast Guard rating that specializes in performing administrative, correspondence, payroll, and other clerical tasks. A "Yeoman First Class" (YN1) is one paygrade and rank higher than a "Yeoman Second Class" (YN2).

"Flood": In U.S. Coast Guard and Navy practice, ship names are written in all-capitals. Commissioned in 1969, U.S. Coast Guard Hamilton-class cutter MORGANTHAU (WHEC-722) served for 48 years, including a 1970-1971 mission in Vietnamese waters, until it was decommissioned in 2017.

"Hamilton": The U.S. Coast Guard celebrates as its birthday Aug. 4,

1790, the date on which then-Secretary of the Treasury Alexander Hamilton successfully urged Congress to authorize the construction of 10 small ships called "revenue cutters," for the purpose of enforcing U.S. tariff laws under the U.S. Constitution.

"Heroes": At the time of this writing, Douglas Albert Munro (1919-1942) is the sole member of the U.S. Coast Guard to have been awarded the Medal of Honor, the U.S. military's highest medal. Signalman First Class Munro was killed Sept. 27, 1942 during the Guadalcanal Campaign, while leading an extraction of U.S. Marines who had been overrun by Japanese troops. Munro piloted his Higgins boat to shield another such craft that was filled with Marines, when he was struck down by gunshot.

"Identity": As an organization responsible for collecting revenue, the Coast Guard was part of the Department of Treasury from 1790 until 1967. At that time, the organization was moved to the Department of Transportation. After the terrorist attacks of September 11, 2001, the Coast Guard became one of the original member organizations of the Department of Homeland Security (DHS) in 2003.

A "plank-owner" is any crewmember who served with the initial crew of a newly commissioned unit or ship. In this way, anyone who was serving in the Coast Guard when the service transitioned into the new department can be considered a "plank-owner" of DHS.

"Indoctrination": In U.S. military training, "indoctrination" refers to basic training received by most all new recruits. Recruits or enlistees who have prior military service, regardless of previous branch, are described as being "prior-service." An "Officer Candidate School" (O.C.S.) course of instruction, is a months-long course that results in an enlisted member receiving a commission as an entry-level officer. The initialism "DoD," pronounced "dee-oh-dee," refers the U.S. Department of Defense. The initialism "MTV" refers to the American cable TV channel that once specialized in "Music Television."

"Initiation": Seagoing services observe various light-hearted "ceremonies," which commemorate milestones in a servicemember's career while boosting crew morale. Two common examples are earning a title of "Shellback" when an individual crosses the equator aboard ship for the first time, and entering the "Domain of the Golden Dragon" when first crossing the International Dateline, which is located at 180-degrees Longitude.

Before participating in either initiation rite, crewmembers are addressed as "Polliwogs"—a tongue-in-cheek derogatory term. In order to ensure that high-spirited crewmembers don't cross the line into actions that could be considered hazing, however, seasoned leaders occasionally have to step in with some last-minute guidance. Rubbing urinal cakes on people's faces, for example, would not be acceptable.

"Rank Has Its Medals": The Meritorious Service Medal (M.S.M.) is awarded to servicemembers who have distinguished themselves in achievement or service. In the U.S. Coast Guard, the medal is perceived to be reserved for officers with the ranks of commander or captain (O-5 or O-6), or enlisted with the rank of chief petty officer (E-7) or higher. A Coast Guard Commendation Medal is a lower, mid-level award.

"Ring-knockers": Officers who receive their commissions via graduation from one of the U.S. military academies are stereotypically known for their wear and display of their respective class rings. By knocking such a ring against a desk or door, a wearer can call further attention to their status as an academy graduate—a distinction that can be perceived as a privileged, club-like affair.

"Semper Paratus": The motto of the U.S. Coast Guard is "Semper Paratus." (In Latin, the phase means "Always Ready.") The words appear on the official Coast Guard flag. The march of the U.S. Coast Guard, written in 1928, is also titled "Semper Paratus." Reportedly, the phrase can be informally shortened to "Semper P," in a manner similar to colloquially abbreviating the U.S. Marine motto from "Semper Fidelius" ("Always Faithful") to "Semper Fi."

"Shut Up": "In U.S. military training, "indoctrination" refers to basic training received by most all new recruits. Recruits or enlistees who have prior military service, regardless of previous branch, are described as being "prior-service."

"Ski Boat": Capable of making 14 knots (16 mph), the steel-hulled 44-foot Motor Lifeboat was once the standard workhorse of the U.S. Coast Guard rescue fleet. In the late 1990s, it was replaced by an aluminum-hulled 47-foot Motor Lifeboat, capable of making 25 knots (29 mph) maximum and 22 knots (25 mph) cruising.

"Success": One way that people can be commissioned as officers in the U.S. Coast Guard is to graduate from a 17-week Officer Candidate School (O.C.S.) course of instruction. Another way is to graduate from the U.S. Coast Guard Academy or other service academy. In return for receiving a four-year undergraduate education as well as a commission, academy graduates incur obligations to serve as active-duty officers for at least five years.

"360": A "watchstander" is a member of a ship's company who is currently on duty, and tasked with the safe operation, navigation, and direction of that ship.

"National Coast Guard": The U.S. Coast Guard is sometimes confused with the U.S. National Guard. The latter is part of the Reserve Component of the U.S. Armed Forces. As such, a majority of National Guard members are "part-time" citizen-soldiers or -airmen, who are popularly said to fulfill an annual minimum of "one weekend a month, plus two weeks a year" of military training.

"OERs": The initialism refers to Officer Evaluation Reports, which are regularly documented assessments of an officer's job description, performance, and development.

"Organizational Structure": An "E-2" refers to a military pay level. In the U.S. Coast Guard, someone of this pay grade holds the rank titled "Seaman Apprentice." A "chief" is a senior enlisted member, pay grade E-7 and above. The Commandant is the singular commander of the U.S. Coast Guard as an organization.

"On Report": An Executive Officer (XO) is a captain's nominal second-in-command, and is often the day-to-day manager of an organization's human resources, maintenance, and other critical efforts.

"Prior Enlisted": In each branch of the U.S. Armed Forces, the Good Conduct Medal is awarded to enlisted servicemembers who have completed three consecutive years without disciplinary action. Only officers who have received the medal while enlisted can achieve and wear the award.

"Uniform Gedunk": The slang term "Gedunk" (pronounced GHEE-dunk") refers to junk foods such as ice cream, candy, and potato chips purchased at a snack bar or canteen. In the U.S. Army, Navy, and Marines, qualified servicemembers awarded the parachutist badge, also known as "jump wings," can display that emblem on both duty and dress uniforms. In the U.S. Army, only soldiers who hold Infantry job specialties who have also engaged in combat are eligible for the Combat Infantryman Badge (C.I.B.).

"Warrant Officers": Warrant officers are a class of highly specialized, single-track technicians. They can perform command duties, but are more often assigned to fill positions of technical expertise. The ranks fall between that of enlisted and commissioned officers.

A FEW WORDS OF THANKS

I am less a "warrior-poet" and more a "storyteller with a military background." That said, however, I have to acknowledge the influences that have swirled into my work. Of course, Wilfred Owen's World War I poetry is in there, but so is the work of Keith Douglas in World War II. Also Leroy Quintana's book of Vietnam experiences, *Interrogations*.

I grew up in South Central Kentucky listening to the local, culture-based perspectives on being human, and picked up on humor and matter-of-fact world-views there that could never be denied. With their stories of church-like stoicism and hard farm work—along with others both hilarious and sublime (like the time a 40-pound gopher got sucked into a Coke bottle during a tornado)—the people of Kentucky were always worth listening to. They were fundamental to my early development as a writer.

And, what poet shouldn't thank his family? Katrina and the boys have rarely known me to be without a pen and a journal writing down notes and poems to the universe. So I thank them for letting me be my most authentic self. I hope they appreciate *Always Ready* more than any other readers.

Thanks to Jacquelyn Bengfort, U.S. Navy veteran, writer of poetry and fiction, and author of the micro-chapbooks *Navy News Service* and *Suitable for All Methods of Communication* (Ghost City Press). Bengfort understands that fairy tales start off with "once upon a time ..." but sea stories start off with "hey, this is no S--- ..." Lucky for us, some sea stories are actually worth (re)telling!

Thanks to Randy Brown, editor-publisher at Middle West Press LLC and fellow military storyteller, for helping give voice to the shared humanity that sparks across veteran experiences—and transcends thank-you-for-your-service sentiments. Together, we can make our military pasts come alive and fight the stereotyped zombies of having served.

Thanks to U.S. Navy veteran and physician Frederick Foote for his particular notice of family themes in my poetry. Beyond the exciting tales of boats, cutters, and helicopters there are always other stories hovering over the fates of our loved ones—civilians who have been made to tag along, voluntarily or involuntarily, on our lives of service. Family members go along for the whole cruise, put up with a lot of organizational decisions with which they might disagree, and (sometimes) hit Bingo Fuel before the end.

Thanks to Sonner Kehrt, U.S. Coast Guard veteran and now an investigative reporter at *The War Horse Journal*, for her insightful endorsement of *Always Ready*, based on our mutual experiences in "country's least-known military service." I have been retired too long for our paths to have crossed while either of us was in uniform, but change can be slow, particularly at sea. I'm sure we've seen some of the same things, just in different times and ports.

Thanks to U.S. Navy veteran Daniel Charles Ross, author of *Force No One* and other military thrillers, for his kind words regarding my intent to help enrich the U.S. Coast Guard story. Beyond consuming popular Coast Guard-themed movies such as "Onionhead" (1958), "The Guardian" (2006), and "The Finest Hours" (2016), the public is often left with little else on which to secure their appreciation of the service. Action-packed thrillers are just one tool. Poetry is another!

Thanks to Caroline Walsh, U.S. Coast Guard veteran and author of the memoir *Fairly Smooth Operator: My Life Occasionally at the Tip of the Spear* (Koehler Books), for appreciating the deeper intentions behind these poems. In telling our service stories in new ways, we help document the ingenuity and humor it takes to maneuver an organization through troubled times, missions, and waters. *Semper Paratus!*

ABOUT THE WRITER

Benjamin B. White once dreamt of joining Cincinnati's "Big Red Machine" as a centerfielder. He played baseball in high-school, junior college, university, and even in the German-American *Bundeslinga*, before a worn-out shoulder changed his life's course.

After an enlistment in the U.S. Army, White ended up as an officer in the United States Coast Guard.

White graduated Coast Guard indoctrination training at Cape May, New Jersey. Newly married, he and his wife Katrina drove a pick-up truck to Alameda, California, where White was assigned to the USCG Cutter Morganthau. He spent nine of the next fourteen months away from home.

The marriage weathered that first tour, and the couple moved on to duty stations in Cape May, New Jersey; Washington, D.C.; Seattle, Washington; New Orleans, Louisiana; East Moriches, New York.

White holds undergraduate degrees in creative writing and philosophy from the University of New Mexico; a Master of Business Administration from the City University of Seattle; a Master of Fine Arts in poetry writing from University of Tampa, Florida; and, finally, both a graduate degree in educational technology leadership and a doctorate in human and organizational learning from George Washington University.

Now retired from uniformed service, White teaches business administration courses for Central New Mexico Community College; human resources courses for the University of Maryland Global Campus; and Career and College Success courses for the Southwest Indian Polytechnic Institute (SIPI).

White's military-themed poems have appeared in such literary venues as Military Experience & the Arts' *As You Were*, and Southeast Missouri State University's *Proud to Be: Writing from American Warriors* anthologies. His previous books include *Buddha Bastinado Blues*; *Conley Bottom: A Poemoir*; and *The Recon Trilogy +1*. White is also acquisitions editor for Running Wild Press LLC, Los Angeles.

DID YOU ENJOY THIS BOOK?

Tell your friends and family about it! Post your thoughts via social media sites, like Facebook, Instagram, and Twitter!

You can also share a quick review on websites for other readers, such as Goodreads.com. Or offer a few of your impressions on bookseller websites, such as Amazon.com and BarnesandNoble.com!

Recommend the title to your favorite local library, poetry society or book club, museum gift store, or independent bookstore!

There is nothing more powerful in business of publishing than a shared review or recommendation from a friend.

We appreciate your support! We'll continue to look for new stories and voices to share with our readers. Keep in touch!

You can write us at:

Middle West Press LLC
P.O. Box 1153
Johnston, Iowa 50131-9420

Or visit: www.middlewestpress.com

September Eleventh:
an epic poem, in fragments
by Amalie Flynn

Permanent Change of Station and *FORCES*
by Lisa Stice

Made in the USA
Monee, IL
17 August 2022

The
WHITE CLIFFS
of DOVER

To Fay

Thanks for your help

Best wishes,

from Paul

PAUL HARRIS

12/9/14

AMBERLEY

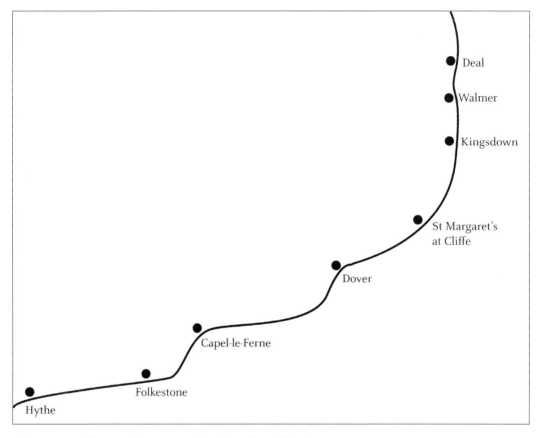

A basic map of the coastal area covered in *The White Cliffs of Dover*.

First published 2013

Amberley Publishing
The Hill, Stroud
Gloucestershire, GL5 4EP

www.amberley-books.com

Copyright © Paul Harris, 2013

The right of Paul Harris to be identified as the Author
of this work has been asserted in accordance with the
Copyrights, Designs and Patents Act 1988.

ISBN 978 1 4456 1887 6 (print)
ISBN 978 1 4456 1866 1 (ebook)

British Library Cataloguing in Publication Data.
A catalogue record for this book is available from the
British Library.

Typesetting by Amberley Publishing.
Printed in the UK.

Contents

Acknowledgements

I would like to thank all those who have helped this publication to see the light of day by providing photographs, information, advice, suggestions and practical assistance. I am particularly grateful to Ian Pakeman and Candida Wright for supplying so many photographs to help illustrate this book, Tony and Debbie at the Little Switzerland Camping Site for showing me 'their' colony of wall lizards, Alan Taylor for supplying the old photograph of cattle grazing at the Warren in chapter 3, Kirk Alexander of White Cliffs Countryside Partnership for supplying information and pictures for use in chapters 3, 4 and 5, Group Captain Patrick Tootal of the Battle of Britain Memorial Trust for allowing me to use the emotive poem 'Our Wall' in chapter 4, Kent Libraries and Archives, and particularly the staff at the Peter Davies Heritage Room in Folkestone Library, for providing images from their collection also for use in chapter 4, Linda Mewes and Bryan Williams for sorting out images of two paintings by W. H. Prior and one of the Bronze Age Boat for use in chapter 5, Dr Peter Burville for allowing me quotes from his excellent book *The White Cliffs of Dover: Images of Cliff and Shore*, along with permission to reproduce a painting by Samuel Gillespie Prout, of a former Dover cave dwelling, also in chapter 5, artist Diana Harrison for allowing reproduction of her fine painting of a cliff view of South Foreland facing chapter 6, Chris Raines of Copylink for providing printouts of my work at short notice and affordable prices, and of course Amberley Publishing for commissioning me in the first place and producing the final work you see before you. Finally, I would like to thank my partner Candida for her continued advice, support and encouragement, and John Webber, whose invaluable, practical help ensured that this project was successfully completed on time.

If I have omitted to credit anyone correctly for any material that appears in this book, please accept my apologies. If you contact either myself or the publisher we will ensure any corrections appear in future editions of this book.

Introduction

Having lived most of my life on the Kent Coast I have naturally become very familiar with the 18 miles of spectacular coastline running from Folkestone to Deal, most of which has become known across the world as the White Cliffs of Dover.

As a child, I played in and explored the wilderness of Folkestone Warren for most of the long summer holidays. Sometimes I would net newts in a seasonal pond and other times I would explore rock pools for crabs, or search where the cliff faces met the shore for fossils. Later, as a teenager, I explored the remaining wartime structures, both above and below ground that were, and to some extent still are, to be found on and in these cliffs. In my thirties I became a keen walker, walking the length of the cliffs in one go or covering shorter stretches, all the while becoming increasingly aware of the area's special wildlife, history, folklore and literary associations.

Semi-retirement saw me as a Martello tower custodian and later as assistant manager of the local visitor information centre. In both places I would speak to interested visitors and passing locals, and find myself answering many of their questions.

Alongside these 'day jobs', I developed a paying hobby writing articles and books, on subjects relating to the coastline which I have become so familiar. However, when researching for my writing I found much of what I read unsatisfying. General guides to the coast and particularly walking guides are useful for the directions, contact numbers and hard data they contain but did little to inspire armchair travellers to make the real journey and explore this coast for themselves. Consequently, when I came to write this book I determined that although it would contain interesting facts, figures and background information within the text, it would not be primarily a guide but more a celebration. I have endeavoured therefore to additionally furnish the curious potential visitor with the sort of quirky stories and information that local people tend to know about and that don't always make it to the average encyclopaedic guidebook.

The White Cliffs of Dover has been arranged as a geographical journey from west to east and then north, following the shoreline, keeping the sea to the right though not designed specifically as a walk. Why keep the sea to my right you might ask and not go in the other direction? That is a good question and can only be answered by saying that it is my personal preference, I always tend to walk coastlines with the sea to my right. This might be something to do with having the prevailing wind at my back or walking towards the rising morning sun, or perhaps some other psychological or subliminal physical reason I have yet to determine. Of course you, the reader, might like to follow the coast in the opposite direction, moving south and then west, with the sea to your left – take your pick; hopefully my book will still be useful to you.

However you decide to travel along the White Cliffs of Dover, my hope is that this book provides an inspiring flavour of this iconic coastline, its nature, history and atmosphere, and that this encourages exploration by the appreciative visitor and local resident alike.

Paul Harris, Folkestone

1

The White Cliff Coast

The stretch of cliffs from Folkestone to Walmer on the Kent coast, known across the world as the White Cliffs of Dover, is perhaps England's most iconic natural feature. It is also among the most historically significant coastlines in the country.

Generations of returning travellers have found them a welcoming sight. I have heard an audible sigh of relief from weary cross-channel ferry passengers as the cliffs come into view on the approach to Dover Harbour.

The distinctive white of the cliffs is, of course, down to their being composed of chalk; a sedimentary rock laid down during the Cretaceous period between 80 and 64 million years ago, at the rate of about 1 cm every 1,000 years. Chalk is actually made up of billions upon billions of tiny sea shells called 'coccoliths', which accumulated at the bottom of the warm, shallow sea that covered this area at the time. Later, the same geological movements that created the Alps uplifted the old Cretaceous seabed into a series of folds, so forming the basis of an extensive chalk downland. Until around 8,000 years ago, a broad river valley cut through this downland. Then, as sea levels rose at the end of the last ice age, the valley was flooded and became what we now know as the English Channel. A reminder of those days has been found under the sea just off Folkestone: a sudden drop in the seabed where a waterfall once tumbled, with the accumulated gravel of a plunge pool at its base, is evidence of the river that once flowed where now there is only sea. Since that time, the sea has continued to erode the coastline, causing the landslips and rock falls that have created the chalk cliffs we see today. The White Cliffs of Dover, then, can really be said to date from the creation of the Channel.

By this time, human beings were already here, and they continued to arrive, only now by sea instead of on foot. Many were traders, and a boat that sunk over 3,500 years ago just off this coast with a cargo of axes and other goods is preserved in Dover Museum. As well as traders came settlers, waves of them, each bringing their own distinctive culture, knowledge and skills: farming, pottery making and the use of bronze and iron among them. Human intercourse in all its forms spread from here inland, along a network of ancient footpaths that run along the crests of the downs, converging on Salisbury Plain, Stonehenge and Avebury. Here and at other points along the way, other tracks that could take the travellers west, north or east could be joined. Evidence of this widespread travel and trade is plentiful. For instance, identical gold cups of Bronze Age vintage have been found in burial sites at Rillaton in Cornwall and Ringlemere in Kent, quern (milling) stones made on the shore at Folkestone have been found in what is today Northamptonshire, and identical bronze swords dating to 700 BC have been discovered at East Wear Bay in Kent and Weymouth Bay in Dorset. Not only traders and settlers came, but also invaders.

Julius Caesar is said to have made landfall in 55 BC at Walmer. Since then there have been Saxons, Vikings and Normans, papal representatives, threats from Napoleonic France and attacks by Hitler's Luftwaffe. Naturally, this coastline has become well fortified, and even today it is still peppered with Roman remains, medieval castles, Tudor forts, Martello towers, sound mirrors, gun emplacements, pillboxes, radar masts and abandoned nuclear shelters. New arrivals are still coming, with the Channel Tunnel and Dover Harbour being principal points of entry.

Such an important stretch of coastline could not fail to be well visited, and tourists today are well catered for with a host of interesting visitor attractions that just add to the lure of the cliffs themselves. The White Cliffs of Dover are designated a Heritage Coast, and some of this also falls within the Kent Downs Area of Outstanding Natural Beauty (AONB). Several sections are either Sites of Special Scientific Interest (SSSI), Local Nature Reserves, or belong to the National Trust. The latter, along with the White Cliffs Countryside Partnership (WCCP), do a commendable job in managing much of this superb coastal landscape. Walkers, too, are well catered for. The old trackways mentioned earlier have become the long-distance footpaths known as the North Downs Way, the Pilgrims Way and the Saxon Shore Way. The first two (partially identical) will take you along the Folkestone to Dover stretch of the coast, the latter all the way to Walmer and beyond.

More recently, a walking and cycle route (part of Sustrans National Cycle Route 2) called the Chalk and Channel Way has been created. This runs from Folkestone to Dover connecting the two harbours. It is punctuated at intervals by relevant artworks, perhaps the most intriguing of which is the sculpture by Tim Clapcott, situated on the downs behind Folkestone, depicting the previously mentioned coccoliths, which are, of course, responsible for it all in the first place.

This book is a journey along and a celebration of this most loved of English landscapes. Starting in the west where the North Downs meet the sea and become the chalk cliffs, just east of Folkestone, our journey takes us through the wonderful undercliff at Folkestone Warren, along the battle scarred clifftops of Capel-le-Ferne, to where the Channel Tunnel leaves our shores and ships criss-cross what is said to be the world's busiest shipping lane. On to the mighty Dover Castle with its fascinating history (and maybe ghosts!), the lighthouse where Marconi carried out the first cross-Channel radio transmissions, and the bay beyond where Channel swimmers set off for France and Ian Fleming penned the adventures of Double-O agent James Bond. Finally, we descend the cliffs at Kingsdown to Walmer Castle, home of the Lord Warden of the Cinque Ports, and reach the end of our journey.

But that is all to come, let us now start at the beginning.

Opposite above: The start of the cliffs, showing Martello towers above East Wear Bay. (*Photograph by Ian Pakeman, 1995*). *Opposite below*: East Wear Bay shoreline. (*Author's photograph*). *Opposite inset*: Coccoliths sculpture by Tim Clapcott, on the Chalk and Channel Way. (*Author's photograph*)

2

East Wear Bay

Our journey along the historic 16 miles of the White Cliffs of Dover starts just east of the seaside resort of Folkestone, on the gault clay headland known as Copt Point. From here the chalk cliffs marching eastwards are clearly visible. Behind us, to the west, the lower greensand, East Cliff descends towards Folkestone.

View Over Folkestone

The view from Copt Point captures a large chunk of the town, with residential streets in the foreground and the sandy bathing beach and fishing harbour beyond. A long harbour wall with a newly refurbished lighthouse at the end is testament to Folkestone's former role as a busy port. Folkestone Harbour was the first to run cross-Channel ferries to the Continent upon the coming of the railway in 1843. Later, during the First World War, it became the main port for troops leaving for or returning from the battlefields of Europe. An incredible 7 million are said to have passed through here. Next year will see a number of commemorative events take place in the town and the erection of a memorial in the form of an archway over the road down which the troops marched, many, sadly, never to return.

Not only troops but refugees passed through this port. No less than 64,500 arrived here from Belgium from August 1914 onwards. Many subsequently settled locally or elsewhere in the country. A painting by former refugee Fredo Franzoni of this mass arrival being greeted by the town's dignitaries has recently been restored, and hangs in the ballroom of The Grand, a former hotel, now turned into flats, a restaurant and entertainment venue. The Grand is a superb Edwardian building situated on The Leas, which is a 1½-mile-long stretch of clifftop grassland to the west of the town.

It was in The Grand that Edward VIII entertained his mistress Alice Keppel on his visits to Folkestone in the 1900s. It was also where Agatha Christie wrote part of her famous novel *Murder on the Orient Express*.

Elsewhere on The Leas are other points of interest. At the western end is a viewpoint into the moat of an ivy-covered Martello tower. The tunnel through the foliage to the viewpoint is in fact one of the Folkestone Artworks, a collection of contemporary art situated in public spaces around the town. This example is called *Towards the Sound of Wilderness*, and was created by artist Cristina Iglesias. Near the restored bandstand is another example: *Folk Stones* by Mark Wallinger. This consists of a rectangular area paved with 19,240 pebbles, each one numbered, one for every person who died in the first day of the Battle of the Somme in 1916. Among other such artworks can also be seen a life-size mermaid sculpture modelled on local woman Georgina Baker, by artist Cornelia Parker. This overlooks the sandy beach known as Sunny Sands near the harbour. These and many other works were commissioned for the three-yearly Folkestone Triennial, an exhibition of contemporary art.

Above: View over Folkestone from Copt Point. (*Author's photograph*)

Right: Mermaid sculpture at the Sunny Sands, by Cornelia Parker. (*Author's photograph*)

The first two were in 2008 and 2011, with a third due in 2014. After each Triennial, a number of works are retained in the town on a permanent basis, building up a local collection.

The other main festival the town has is the Folkestone Festival, which occurs every June and sometimes includes the ever-popular Folkestone Airshow, which can bring in 100,000 visitors over a weekend.

As for the harbour, cross-Channel ferries finally ceased in 2002, a victim of the coming of the Channel Tunnel and the ending of cross-Channel duty-free sales. The Channel Tunnel terminal lies outside the town to the west, and so outside of the scope of this book, though we will cross paths with the tunnel elsewhere later.

But, enough of the attractions of Folkestone, our way lies east along the cliffs.

Crumbling Cliffs, Fossils and Marine Life

The headland on the East Cliff, from where we have our view of Folkestone in one direction and the chalk cliffs toward Dover in the other, is composed of gault clay on a bedrock of lower greensand and surmounted by a 'knob' of chalk. The soft clay easily erodes in heavy rain and crumbles or turns into liquid mudflows that pour onto the beach below. In my childhood, a road ran around the edge of the cliff here, but a landslip in 1988 carried this away and now there is no sign that it ever existed.

These crumbling cliffs expose many Cretaceous fossils of marine creatures such as belemites, which are the fossilised bodies of tiny squids and appear as shiny, bullet-shaped objects, and ammonites, those most beautiful of fossils, intricate, coiled shells that were also once home to a form of nautilus or squid. These can sometimes be composed of iron pyrite and exhibit iridescent colours, as perhaps their shells displayed in life. Fossil hunters from across the world come here for field studies. Many of the finest examples of some ammonite

Above and opposite: Cliff erosion and the end of the road at the East Cliff, *c.* 1988. (*Author's photographs*)

Ammonites preserved in iron pyrite. (*Author's photographs*)

species, such as euhoplites truncatus, euhoplites latus and euhoplites planus, have been found here. However, fossil hunting can be rather hazardous, since the difficult, rocky terrain can easily lead to twisted ankles, broken bones or worse. Deep mudflows can trap the unwary and could completely swallow a child. Also, as with many shorelines beneath cliffs, there is the ever present threat of being cut off by the tide.

The rocks, between which many of these fossils can be found, extend out in a vast expanse at low tide. They are mostly covered in seaweed, with substantial rock pools in places. Copt Point is considered to be the most extensive and important such habitat in south-east England. The rock pools are interesting to explore for the marine life they hold, including a variety of crabs, sea snails and sea anemones. At high tide, the seaweed here is suspended by the water to create a seaweed forest among which fish swim, anemones open, brittle stars abound and sometimes, in the late summer, seals forage. Both grey and common seals have been seen around these rocks.

Winter sees the mass arrival of Mediterranean gulls. Observers from the Royal Society for the Protection of Birds (RSPB) and the Sandwich Bay Bird Observatory Trust (SBBOT) have counted between 100 and 200 of these birds here at any one time, compared to a mere five or six at other sites along the Kent coast. Mediterranean gulls, despite their name, come from far and wide, many from France or Eastern Europe, as well as further south. Many have been ringed so their movements are known. One bird in particular seems to migrate specifically between Folkestone and Barcelona each year.

Martello Towers

On the green hilltop of Copt Point there are a number of interesting features, each with its own story to tell. The squat, round, cream-painted tower overlooking the pitch and putt course is a Martello tower. Two others can be seen to the north, both of which have been converted into private dwellings. These are all part of a chain of seventy-four such towers built along the South Coast between Folkestone and Seaford, Sussex, between 1805 and 1812, as a defence against an expected invasion by Napoleonic France. The towers in this vicinity are the first three of the chain, the cream-painted tower being number three. This is currently empty, but was formerly a visitor centre dealing with local history and that of Martello towers generally.

Each of these towers is composed of over a half a million bricks, and has walls that are 8 feet thick on their land-facing side and an incredible 13 feet thick on the seaward side (from where an attack might be expected). They were each surmounted by a cannon swivelling around on a rail that could fire a 1-lb shot for a mile, and could hold twenty-four troops. When Napoleon failed to arrive, the Martello towers were converted to other uses or left empty. During the early nineteenth century, this tower held troops acting as a preventative force to combat the smuggling that was rife along this coast at the time. Following this, a succession of coastguard families lived here. A drawing of Martello Tower No. 3 done for S. J. Mackie's book *Folkestone and its Neighbourhood*, published in 1883, illustrates this.

Martello No. 3 has a more modern room constructed on the top, which dates from the Second World War. A naval unit was housed here initially, which would have able to detonate a line of mines outside Folkestone Harbour in the event of Hitler's forces attempting a landing. Later in the war, the Royal Observer Corps (ROC) took up residence.

Coastwatch Lookout

Near the tower are two other significant wartime relics: a large bunker that once belonged to the Admiralty and a number of strange concrete and metal protrusions from an underground Cold War nuclear bunker. The large bunker was empty for decades after the Second World War, until a nearby coastguard hut had to be demolished due to its imminent break up caused by cliff erosion. By this time, HM Coastguard no longer manned this post but the National Coastwatch Institution (NCI) did. After a couple of unsatisfactory temporary arrangements and a monumental fundraising task, the NCI, which is an entirely voluntary body, was able to take over the bunker and use it for visual watchkeeping duties. Here, trained volunteers keep watch along this stretch of coast, which is a blind spot for HM Coastguard, who are situated 8 miles away, beyond Dover. They look out for any vessel in distress, drifting inflatable boats and lilos, swimmers in difficulty, walkers falling down the cliffs, and other unfortunate accidents. The Coastguard, lifeboat, fire brigade, Search and Rescue helicopter or air ambulance can then be summoned if thought necessary, and directed as appropriate. This branch of NCI were awarded the Queen's Award for Voluntary Service by the Lord Lieutenant of Kent, and presented to proud station manager Tony Hutt at a ceremony on 7 October 2011.

Royal Observer Corps Post

The nuclear bunker was occupied until the late 1960s by the ROC. During the Cold War, this organisation evolved from its aircraft-spotting role held in the Second World War to that of detecting nuclear blasts and their location and measuring their intensity, along with wind speed and direction. This information would then be communicated by landline telephone to a control centre where emergency procedures (evacuation, etc.) could be coordinated. This

Martello Tower No. 3. (*Author's photograph*)

Drawing of Martello Tower No. 3, 1883.

Coastwatch station with old ROC bunker in the foreground, 2012. (*Author's photograph*)

was to be done in the event of a nuclear attack, by small groups of observers holed up in a network of underground bunkers across the country, deploying and reading instruments outside the bunker. Each bunker was supplied with enough dried food and drinking water to last six observers two weeks, by which time it was assumed the emergency might be over.

Protruding above the surface from the Copt Point bunker are the entrance hatchway and air filter, a main air filter housing and metal post upon which measuring instruments would be affixed. These would consist of a photosensitive recorder, weather vane and anemometer.

This particular ROC post was abandoned due to coastal erosion in the late 1960s and replaced with one up on the Downs behind Folkestone. The ROC itself was disbanded at the end of the Cold War in the early 1990s and the bunkers sold off or left derelict.

Roman Villa Site

To the north of Copt Point, the land levels out into a grassy, clifftop recreational area under which lie the buried remains of a substantial Roman villa. A nearby noticeboard has full pictorial information. The villa was discovered in 1923 by schoolteacher Mr S. E. Winbolt, who hastily arranged a full excavation the following year. The site was left on view to the public until 1954 when it was decided that, to protect it from weather damage and souvenir hunters, it would be best to bury it once again.

Since then, the cliff edge has moved gradually inland and parts of the former villa have disappeared. This has led to an urgent need to fully research what is there before it is lost forever. With this in mind, excavation of the former bath house was carried out in 1989. More recently, a project called A Town Unearthed (ATU) coordinated by Canterbury Christ Church University and the Canterbury Archaeological Trust undertook two years of major re-excavation of parts of this site in 2010 and 2011, with some follow-up work in 2012.

Excavation work on the Roman villa site at
East Wear Bay, 2012. (*Author's photographs*)

These new excavations uncovered abundant evidence of Iron Age settlement of this site, which was eventually occupied by the Roman villa. During the second century, the villa fell into ruins, but was replaced by new buildings in the third century. Coin finds suggest these buildings may have been in use until at least AD 390, after which the site seems to have been abandoned.

Many interesting finds were made as a result of the ATU excavations. These included a beautiful second-century Roman copper alloy brooch in the likeness of a hare and also many milling stones called 'querns', some dating back to the Iron Age.

The latter confirmed earlier evidence that substantial numbers of these stones were made locally. Many of the stones were exported far and wide, some from Folkestone having been found as far away as Northamptonshire. Although it seems quern export ceased at the end of the Roman period, more general stone export for use in sea and harbour walls continued until at least the times of Oliver Cromwell, according to eighteenth-century historian Edward Hasted.

ATU was named 'Rescue Dig of the Year' in the Current Archaeology Awards in 2013 for their work at East Wear Bay. Two books explaining the project and its findings were published in 2013 and launched at the Folkestone Book Festival.

Sword in the Sea

Below this important archaeological site lies the wild, undeveloped shoreline of East Wear Bay. Here the gault clay cliffs collapse onto the sandy seashore, sometimes bringing with them items of archaeological interest from the site above. Pieces of Roman pottery, tiles and even the occasional gold coin have been found over the years. Lumps of ironstone that can be seen both emerging from the cliffs and scattered about on the beach are natural in origin. Some of this local ironstone was used in the construction of the walls of the Roman villa.

Perhaps the most interesting historical find here was a bronze sword dredged up about 40 yards offshore by a Mr H. Brice while out fishing in his boat in the spring of 1951. The sword was noticed at the fish market when the day's catch was being landed, and was subsequently brought to the attention of the archaeological world by a Mr G. Finn of Hythe. A full report was published by the Kent Archaeological Society in 1952, where comparison was made with a virtually identical sword, one of two discovered in a stream running into the sea near Weymouth in Dorset. Similar swords have been found in the River Thames and feature in an interesting display at the River and Rowing Museum at Henley-on-Thames. This type of sword is usually dated to as far back as 700 BC, when it was common practice to throw such items into bodies of water as votive offerings. It may be that this practice was the basis for the legend that King Arthur's sword Excalibur was thrown into a lake at the end of his life, as written down in the much later Arthurian stories.

Sea Wall and 'Apron'

From the wild shoreline of East Wear Bay, a sea wall punctuated by concrete groynes stretches away to the east, culminating in two large concrete platforms known as 'aprons'. These form part of attempts by Network Rail to maintain the Folkestone to Dover railway line, which has historically been subject to disruption from landslips. The railway was built in the 1840s through the undercliff known as The Warren (see Chapter 3), which lies between the cliffs and the sea. As early as 1877, the line had to be closed due to major rock falls. Then on 19 December 1915, a major cliff fall along the whole line of the cliffs behind the railway took place. A train was left stranded on the contorted railway line, and troops were deployed to lead the trapped passengers off the train and back to safety through a railway tunnel to Folkestone. The railway remained closed for over two years until 1918 when repairs were completed.

'Apron' at East Wear Bay, a 'toe weight' to hold back the forward movement of the cliffs. (*Author's photograph*)

To combat the ever-present possibility of a repeat of such events, British Rail undertook a major stabilisation project between 1948 and 1953. This consisted of the current sea wall to prevent undercutting by the sea, the concrete 'aprons' to act as 'toe weights' and hold back the cliff's natural propensity to move gradually seaward, and a series of over twenty drainage tunnels to siphon off the water accumulating underground between the chalk and the gault clay. The latter would minimise the risk of the cliffs sliding on the gault and causing landslips. Since that time, more drainage tunnels have been added, reefs of rocks have been piled up beneath some sections of cliff, and an electronic warning system along the railway line set up. All this has led to this becoming one of, if not the most expensive stretches of railway line to maintain in the country.

The first of the 'aprons' is popularly believed to have had some role in the Second World War as some kind of landing stage, but this is merely local legend as the structure was built later. It does, however, have a couple of historical claims to fame.

Firstly, on 12 June 1979, the first man-powered flight across the Channel took place from here. The flimsy aircraft *Gossamer Albatross*, designed by Paul MacCready and pedalled by cyclist Bryan Allen, made it across in 2 hours 45 minutes. The achievement netted MacCready, Allen and their team £100,000, which had been put up by the industrialist Henry Kremer. No one, to my knowledge, has tried to repeat or better this, so I guess it was very hard work!

Secondly, on 16 October 1987, the car ferry *Hengist*, tossed by heavy seas in the infamous hurricane (that BBC weatherman Michael Fish will never be able to forget he assured us was not coming), broke its moorings in Folkestone Harbour and was stranded on this 'apron'.

A crew remained on board the *Hengist* for several days to prevent attempts at boarding and looting until it could be refloated.

Between the sea wall and the chalk cliffs behind lies the notable undercliff known as The Warren or Folkestone Warren. It is this we will look at in the next chapter.

Car ferry *Hengist* stranded after the 1987 hurricane. (*Copyright Ian Pakeman, 1987*)

3

Folkestone Warren

Folkestone Warren is an area of vegetated undercliff between the high chalk cliffs and the sea. Over the years, rotational landslips have carried sections of the cliffs down toward the sea, so forming an extensive shelf ending in a secondary, lower line of cliffs above the shoreline. This shelf has become colonised by grass, scrub and woodland to form a varied landscape hosting a rich mixture of flora and fauna, including some rare species.

Geographically, the whole undercliff appears on Ordnance Survey maps as 'The Warren', owned partially by Railtrack (who maintain the Dover to Folkestone main line railway that runs along part of the undercliff) and Shepway District Council (SDC), the local authority for Folkestone, Hythe and Romney Marsh. The part owned by SDC is a local nature reserve called the East Cliff & Warren Country Park. The whole of the coast from Copt Point to Samphire Hoe near Dover (of which there is more in the next chapter) is the Folkestone Warren Site of Special Scientific Interest (SSSI), designated as such because of its interesting geology and wildlife.

The famous author H. G. Wells, best known for his early science fiction stories such as *The Time Machine* and *War of the Worlds*, lived at Sandgate near Folkestone from 1898 to 1909. He mentions Folkestone Warren in his classic novel *Kipps: The Story of a Simple Soul*, published in 1905 and subsequently made into the musical play and film *Half a Sixpence*. In this we read of the main character, Arthur Kipps, going for a walk: '...over the East Cliff and into that queer little wilderness of slippery and tumbling clay and rock under the chalk cliffs, a wilderness of thorn and bramble, wild rose and wayfaring tree, that adds so greatly to Folkestone's charm.'

The Warren can essentially be divided into two halves, north of the railway line, below the high chalk cliffs, and south of the line, down towards East Wear Bay. The former I think of as the Upper Warren and the latter as the Lower Warren.

The Lower Warren

This is perhaps the wilder of the two areas, with much scrub and several marshy areas. There are streams and ponds that appear and disappear according to the weather, season and earth movements, and a wealth of lush vegetation and insect life. Horsetails up to 6 feet high, hanging creepers, a woodland carpet of hart's tongue ferns, and an abundance of mosses and lichens combine to create a jungle-like environment. Spring sees stunning primrose displays and on grassy banks in summer, pyramidal, common spotted, lady, bee and late spider orchids can be found. Here and there are newt-filled ponds buzzed over by colourful damsel flies and dragonflies, and in the grass, slow worms, common lizards and grass snakes move swiftly out of harm's way.

Recently, there have been attempts to open up this part of The Warren for the benefit of visitors accessing this natural paradise and to promote greater biodiversity, which suffers if too much scrub, particularly brambles and buddleia, take hold.

Above left: Into Folkestone Warren. *Above right*: Orchids among the horsetails. (*Author's photograph*)

Oakmoss with lichen. (*Author's photograph*)

Primrose display. (*Author's photograph*)

Above left: Hart's tongue fern. *Above right*: Autumn fungi. (*Author's photograph*)

Above left: Woodland path, Folkestone Warren. (*Author's photograph*). *Above right:* East Cliff & Warren Country Park leaflet. Flora of Folkestone Warren. (*WCCP*)

Observations of a Victorian Naturalist

A hundred years or more ago, Folkestone Warren was widely grazed, and also even less stable as the subsequent works to protect the railway had not yet been carried out. Consequently, the area was a much more open landscape. Descriptions of The Warren in those days, along with many wildlife observations, were recorded by local naturalist and headmaster Henry Ullyett in his book *Rambles of a Naturalist Round Folkestone*, published in 1880.

In one diary entry quoted in his book, Ullyett describes a large pond being formed following a landslip in 1877. Two years later in June 1879, he found this pond to be: 'teeming with life both plant and animal, shoals of tadpoles made the water black all around the borders, there must have been thousands of them...' Ullyett goes on to describe dragonflies and damselflies of every hue, and noticed a curious phenomenon: 'I noted, as a fog came creeping from the east over the hills. What a sudden change came over the dragonflies, how inert they became, you could pick them off the leaves with your fingers.' Nearer the sea, just over a ridge, Ullyett found 'another pond filling up a long narrow deep cleft and called the Long Pond'.

The Folkestone Corporation minutes in March 1926 record that a resolution was passed to drain this pond, which was deemed to be dangerous. A later set of the minutes, dated 10 May 1926, record that: '...the dug trench had lowered the pond by 10 feet but that it was still not empty and kept filling up due to its being fed by springs'.

By 20 May, the trench was 20 feet deep and the pond lowered by 12 feet, but was still not empty. On 7 June, a new instruction was issued to fill up the pond so it would not be more

The Long Pond, photograph *c.* 1920. (Taken from the author's book *Folkestone Warren in Old Picture Postcards*, published by European Library in 1993)

than 18 inches deep. This was done, but I think to an adjacent pond that was once well known among anglers for its population of roach. This is now more of a fen and indeed is never more than 18 inches deep, if that!

There are still many small, medium-sized and even one large pond to be found in the Lower Warren today. Some are visible, next to paths, others are hidden away in sheltered glades, hidden treasure houses of wildlife awaiting discovery by those who happen upon them.

Landscape and Habitat Management

The landscape of Folkestone Warren, along with some other areas of coast and countryside around Folkestone and Dover, is managed by the White Cliffs Countryside Partnership (WCCP). They help to conserve the wildlife and landscape with an active management programme of tasks, staffed largely by volunteers under experienced leadership. WCCP is a unique collaboration between local authorities, conservation organisations and local businesses. As well as helping from a conservation point of view, it also provides a wide range of local people with a reason to get out and get fit while enjoying and learning about the countryside. Recently, WCCP have been helped by a Green Gym initiative run by community safety officer Giles Barnard of Shepway District Council (SDC). Kent County Council (KCC) councillor Roland Tolputt used money from his member's grant to provide steps, handrails, footbridges and gravel to help construct a new path from the clifftop to the seashore, while SDC supplied an army of enthusiastic volunteers for the first of the Green Gym projects.

The new pathway was completed in 2012, and Green Gym has continued to work with WCCP on scrub clearance in other parts of Folkestone Warren. WCCP have also

Ponds in the Lower Warren. (*Author's photographs*)

Roland Tolputt (front) and the Green Gym team. (*Author's photograph*)

Giles Barnard (right) working with Green Gym members. (*Author's photograph*)

Above left: New Warren path takes shape, 2011. (*Author's photograph*). *Above right*: A massive chalk fall at Folkestone Warren in 2001 that may have claimed one life. (*Author's photograph*)

reintroduced cattle grazing, which has been absent since being prohibited in 1924 as part of a plan to develop the area for public leisure purposes, following its transference as a gift from the former landowner Lord Radnor. Initially, this will concentrate on a 20-acre area, but may be extended in future. The aim of this is to keep scrub under control and so encourage a wider variety of plants, flowers, insects and other life to flourish in the reinvigorated landscape.

The Upper Warren

North of the railway line is what I think of as the Upper Warren. This is an area of thick woodland, carpeted with hart's tongue ferns beneath the high chalk cliffs. Several paths, some of them quite precipitous, lead down into and through this idyllic, bird-haunted landscape from the village of Capel-le-Ferne above and the camping site, situated in an area halfway up the cliffs known as Little Switzerland. In April, one of these paths is lined by more than a mile of primrose display, leading to its local naming as the Primrose Path. A footbridge across the railway line allows access to the shore. Roughly every thirty years or so, large chalk falls have occurred here; huge chalk boulders tumbling down into the woods and forming great white screes, and sometimes necessitating the rerouting of footpaths or replacing of steps. Within a few years though, vegetation reclaims the tumbled landscape and all seems as it was. On the last such occasion, in 2001, a local man went missing and it is feared that he may have been buried by the rock fall.

Cattle grazing at Folkestone Warren in the 1920s. (*Photograph supplied by Alan Taylor*)

The cliffs here are home to kestrels and also peregrine falcons. The latter are particularly effective birds of prey that are able to dive on and kill their prey with a single blow from their talons, at up to 180 mph. They are said to be the fastest living creature on earth. Kittiwakes are also to be found nesting on impossibly narrow ledges, safely out of reach of any potential predator. An astonishing 1,100 pairs are believed to be nesting along the cliffs between Folkestone and Kingsdown.

Little Switzerland and its Wall Lizards

One of the best viewpoints over this area of The Warren and along the cliffs is at the camping site and café known as Little Switzerland. This is one of two such sites in The Warren, the other being the camping and caravanning site on the shore at East Wear Bay, near the apron mentioned in the previous chapter. Both receive good reviews on the internet by virtue of their superb, scenic positions. Little Switzerland, though, has particularly outstanding views.

An attractive wooden tea chalet was established here in 1924, complete with tea gardens. Unfortunately, this was destroyed by fire during the Second World War, but a replacement chalet, along with a camping site for tents and static caravans, was opened in 1956 and remains very popular.

This is an interesting site from a natural history point of view, since a large population of Italian wall lizards have become established in the vicinity of the campsite and nearby cliff paths. No one is sure where they came from, but some speculate that a local pet shop owner disposed of stock near here, or that the lizards have come in as stowaways in the camper vans of the many European tourists that come to this site every year. The café proprietor says she frequently picks up the lizards, many with a distinctive green-patterned back, and sometimes adders with a litter picker and puts them out of harm's way. Apparently they do not deter customers, with people coming to seek out the reptiles, including university academics and reptile study groups. Full information can be found on the websites of both

Wall Lizard at Little Switzerland, 2013. (*Copyright Candida Wright*)

the Kent Reptile and Amphibian Group (KRAG) and the Surrey Reptile and Amphibian Group (SRAG). These websites claim the population of the lizards is up to 180. However, they produce a very large number of eggs and the campsite owner thinks the number in the immediate area now far exceeds that.

The Warren in Edwardian Times

The Warren, as seen from Little Switzerland, was very popular during the Edwardian period. A railway station called the Warren Halt opened in 1908 and played host to hundreds of visitors every day. They came to ramble, to picnic, to wander to Rakemere Pond, or up the zigzag path to the clifftop village of Capel-le-Ferne and to use a tea chalet that had been erected near the station. Before there were tea chalets in The Warren, people used to stop at one of the eighteen or so cottages that used to exist here. Originally, these had been inhabited by fishermen or smugglers, and later by Coastguard employees and members of the anti-smuggling Preventative Force.

From the 1840s, railway workers, and later those working on sea defences, occupied some of the cottages. The children of the families that lived in The Warren used the train to travel into Folkestone to attend school, disembarking at the former Folkestone East station and walking down Dover or Blackbull Roads to attend St Mary's or Mundella primary schools. By 1914, these cottages had all gone, having succumbed to landslips or been abandoned and lost in the encroaching vegetation. Garden 'escapees' from those days, such as cherry or fig trees, can still be found growing in the area today. The Warren Halt station meanwhile was completely buried in the infamous landslip of 19 December 1915, but was rebuilt and opened again in 1923 for another sixteen years, until another landslip put it out of action. A staff halt for railway workers was, however, reinstated and continued in use for several decades.

From the Little Switzerland campsite, an attractive zigzag cliff path leads up to the clifftop and Capel-le-Ferne, our next port of call.

View from Little Switzerland along the cliffs above Folkestone Warren. (*Author's photograph*)

Modern view of chalet from cliff path. (*Author's photograph*)

The Warren,
Folkestone

*Rakemere Pond (as of now)
Just north of the Station*

Photo Copyright, Burger

Old postcard view of Rakemere Pond, *c.* 1908. (*By kind permission of Kent Libraries & Archives*)

Old postcard view of two of the Warren Cottages. (*By kind permission of Kent Libraries & Archives*)

4

Capel-le-Ferne to Shakespeare Cliff

Capel-le-Ferne, situated some 550 feet above East Wear Bay, has been called the 'village in the clouds', as it is often shrouded in mist and cloud while Folkestone basks in sunshine. The reverse can happen sometimes though, particularly on crisp, calm winter mornings when the village looks down upon low-lying mist or fog, obscuring the landscape below. On these days, it seems a village above the clouds. The name Capel-le-Ferne actually means 'chapel in the ferns', referring to the now redundant St Mary's church, which presumably was once surrounded by ferns. Capel, as it is more often referred to locally, is a mostly modern village with a population of about 2,400.

Ghosts and Smugglers

Coming up the steep Dover Hill from Folkestone, the first building encountered in Capel is the Valiant Sailor public house. It has been known by this name for generations, and was once well known as a staging post for smuggled goods making their way inland after landfall at The Warren. Wherever smuggling is rife, ghost stories seem to arise. Undoubtedly in past – more superstitious times – this would have deterred people from places where smugglers might operate. Today, of course, this would have the opposite effect; attracting thrill-seeking teenagers out on a 'ghost hunt'.

The Valiant Sailor and the footpath along the clifftop to Dover have their fair share of such stories. In the nineteenth century, according to a local newspaper reporter writing under the pseudonym 'Felix' in his book *Rambles around Folkestone*, published in 1913, a ghost 'like a white sheet' was sometimes encountered at a dip in the cliffs called Steddy Hole. At the time, a cliff path came up from The Warren at this point, so smugglers would no doubt have reason to keep people away from here. More recently, I remember as a schoolboy hearing tales of a ghostly abbot and his dog who supposedly patrolled the cliff path between Capel and Abbot's Cliff at night. I don't know when this story started, but it was certainly current in the 1960s. A small tunnel in Abbot's Cliff is still pointed out by some local residents as the 'Abbot's Cave' or 'Hermit's Cave'. It was in fact more likely created as part of a pathway made during the construction of the Folkestone to Dover railway in the 1840s. And come to think of it, I don't remember any stories of anyone claiming to have actually seen this ghostly abbot!

One genuinely old smuggler-related ghost story, however, was republished in the *Folkestone Herald* in December 1934 as 'A Christmas Ghost Story of Old Folkestone'. The

Opposite: Path between Little Switzerland and Capel-le-Ferne, much frequented by wall lizards. (*Author's photograph*)

original author was Bernard Billings, who apparently wrote this down sometime in the late nineteenth century. It relates to the 'Headless Horseman of the Valiant Sailor'. Apparently, so the story goes, a well-known smuggler, a Mr Kingsmill, rented a large house in Dover Road, Folkestone, from which he excavated a tunnel to the seashore. Smuggled goods made their way up this tunnel to the house, and were then transported in the dead of night up to the Valiant Sailor for onward distribution. Kingsmill officially vacated the house after a short time and it subsequently proved impossible to let on account of persistent rumours that it was haunted. The ghost in question was said to be a headless horse ridden by a headless man that had been seen riding between here and the top of the cliffs at Capel.

Rational minds, of course, might be suspicious, and one Lt Sturt (who is historically recorded as being part of the anti-smuggling Preventative Force stationed on this coast during the mid-nineteenth century) certainly was. Not to be frightened by mere ghosts, Sturt eventually apprehended the culprit, who turned out to be none other than Kingsmill. Both he and his horse were covered in flour up to their necks, while their heads were covered in soot. The impression created was of a white horse and rider, both headless! One horse and rider would not carry much contraband, though, so I can only assume that Kingsmill rode the route to frighten away anyone around, and so divert attention away from the activities of his gang.

To the modern mind, this all seems quite far-fetched, but even within the last twenty years there has been a report of the headless horseman of the Valiant Sailor. Presumably, the 'witness' was unaware that this apparition had been found out more than a century earlier! Such is the persistence of folklore!

Moving on along the coast, the next major point of interest is the Battle of Britain Memorial.

The Battle of Britain Memorial

'Never in the field of human conflict was so much owed by so many to so few.' These immortal words, originally spoken by Prime Minister Winston Churchill at the end of the Battle of Britain in 1940, carved in stone, greet the visitor to the national memorial to this most significant event in British history.

Leaflets at the small café and information centre (soon to be complemented by a large state-of-the-art multimedia visitor centre) describe the memorial as: 'A unique place of pilgrimage and reflection at Capel-le-Ferne, Kent, dedicated to the memory of the aircrew who defended this country in the summer and autumn of 1940.'

Built on the site of a Second World War coastal battery, the Battle of Britain Memorial came to be through the efforts of one of 'the few': Wing Commander Geoffrey Page. He believed there should be a single dedicated national memorial to those who had taken part in this pivotal event. Page was a Hurricane pilot who had been shot down and badly burned in the battle. His campaign ultimately led to the unveiling of the Battle of Britain Memorial by Her Majesty Queen Elizabeth the Queen Mother on 10 July 1993.

The central part of the memorial takes the form of an aeroplane propeller (as seen from above) in bricks, in the centre of which sits the impressive statue of an airman gazing out across the Strait of Dover. Around this centrepiece, wreaths are laid during memorial events and commemorations. The statue was carved by Harry Gray of the Carving Workshop, Cambridge. To the north of this stands a curved wall known as the Christopher Foxley-Norris Memorial, which lists the names of the 2,937 airmen who were awarded the Battle of Britain clasp. Christopher Foxley-Norris was a Hurricane pilot who became the first president of the Battle of Britain Memorial Trust.

The significance of this part of the memorial is well articulated in the words of a poem by William Walker of 616 Squadron entitled 'Our Wall', and is one of a book of such poems by Walker, available from the Memorial Information Centre. I have kindly been granted permission by Group Captain Patrick Tootal of the Battle of Britain Memorial Trust to quote the poem in full.

'Our Wall'
Here inscribed the names we knew
Young men with whom we often flew.
Scrambled to many angels high,
They knew that they or their friends might die.
Many were scarcely trained
And many badly burned or maimed.
Behind each name a story lies
Of bravery in summer skies;
Though many brave unwritten tales
Were simply told in vapour trails.
Many now lie in sacred graves
And many rest beneath the waves.
Outnumbered every day they flew,
Remembered here as just 'The Few'.

William L. B. Walker
616 Squadron
Spitfires

'Our Wall' is a poem by the late Flight Lieutenant William Walker and published by the Battle of Britain Memorial Trust. The Trust holds the copyright to the work, which should not be reproduced without permission.

Biographical information on each of the names on the Christopher Foxley-Norris Wall can be found in a substantial volume, which is available to look through on request at the information centre. Further additions to the memorial site include full-scale replicas of a Hurricane Mark 1 and a Spitfire Mark 2a, along with a bust of Air Chief Marshal Sir Keith Park by sculptor Will Davies. Park was the man who commanded 11 Group, Fighter Command, during the Battle of Britain, and has been described as the tactical commander who won the battle.

On the Sunday nearest the 10 July each year, a popular and well attended Memorial Day takes place, which includes a flypast by the Battle of Britain Memorial Flight, consisting of a Lancaster bomber flanked by a Spitfire and a Hurricane. This date is chosen because the Battle of Britain is said officially to have started on the 10 July 1940 and to have been won by the 31 October 1940. The day widely considered, in retrospect, to have been decisive was the 15 September 1940. Something of a tourist attraction now is the opportunity to fly with a Spitfire or Hurricane. Passengers are flown by helicopter alongside one of the wartime planes to watch it manoeuvre at close quarters over the historic White Cliffs country where it all took place. Flights can last from one to three hours, and can be booked online through flywithafighter.com.

Work commenced on a new state-of-the-art visitor centre called 'the Wing' on 9 September 2013, after the project was officially opened by ninety-three-year-old Wing Commander Bob Foster, one of the last of the remaining Few.

Left: Battle of Britain Memorial statue carved by Harry Gray. This was unveiled by Her Majesty Queen Elizabeth the Queen Mother at the official opening of the memorial on 10 July 1993. (*Author's photograph*)

Below: Christopher Foxley-Norris Memorial Wall. (*Author's photograph*)

Right: Bust of Air Chief Marshal Sir Keith Park, by sculptor Will Davies. (*Author's photograph*)

Below: Along the cliffs from Capel. (*Author's photograph*)

Eagle's Nest, where it came to rest after sliding 100 feet down the cliff at Capel-le-Ferne on the evening of 19 December 1915. (*Photograph kindly supplied by Kent Libraries and Archives*)

The House That Moved (Twice)

Further east along the cliffs, just below where you will now find the popular Cliff Top Café, a precipitous footpath descends the wooded cliffs and crosses a footbridge to the sea wall and rocky shore below.

About 60 feet or so down this path there was once a substantial mock Tudor house perched on a ledge, until, that is, nature decided otherwise. Known as Eagle's Nest (not to be confused with a modern house of the same name a mile west of here), this was built in 1911, but didn't stay long. In fact, it moved twice!

The first occasion was during the early evening of 19 December 1915 when the major landslip (mentioned in previous chapters) took place. During the upheaval, Eagle's Nest slid intact 100 feet further down the cliff face before coming to rest.

This major slip disrupted the railway line to Dover, leading to its closure for nearly three years. Meanwhile in Eagle's Nest, the alarmed occupants, Fred and Emma Weston, tried to escape their sliding house but found the doors had warped and stuck in the fall. When the house came to rest, the Westons managed to climb out of a window and struggled down the remainder of the cliff, across screes of tumbled chalk, to arrive in Folkestone five hours later, where they presented themselves at the home of a surprised friend at midnight. However, this was not the end of the mobile career of Eagle's Nest, as a second move was in the offing.

Early in 1916, Epps builders were employed to carefully dismantle the house and haul the pieces up to the clifftop. From here they were transported 17 miles inland to the village of Little Chart near Ashford. Here the house was reassembled and renamed The Sanctuary, secure in its new location.

SSZ 37, from the personal collection of A. R. Purchase. Purchase was the pilot of SSZ 37 in 1918.

A pictorial display of the story of Eagle's Nest was formerly on show at the Cliff Top Café. More information on the Weston's frightening experience can be found in their family history, which has been put into book form and is available to look at in the Heritage Room at Folkestone Library.

Airship Station and the Dover Patrol

Less than a mile further east, we come to the Royal Oak public house. Just next to and behind this there was once an airship station, one of a number built around the coast during the First World War.

The Royal Naval Air Station (RNAS) at Capel had a fleet of nine airships, and commenced operations in 1915 as part of the Dover Patrol. The Dover Patrol's brief was to prevent enemy shipping, mainly submarines or U-boats, from entering the English Channel en route to the Atlantic Ocean. The patrol assembled a large fleet of cruisers, destroyers, armed trawlers and yachts, motor launches, paddle minesweepers, coastal motorboats, submarines, seaplanes, aeroplanes and airships – virtually anything and everything that could be pressed into service. The patrol carried out anti-submarine patrols, escorted merchant, hospital and troop ships, laid sea mines, constructed mine barrages, swept for German mines, bombarded German positions on the Belgian Coast and sunk U-boats. Their most daring exploit was probably the Zeebrugge raid in 1918, which severely damaged Germany's U-boat fleet.

The airships at Capel would look for submarines and alert military surface vessels of their presence so they could be dealt with. The airships used were of the Sea Scout class of non-rigid airships code numbered SSZ. Engineers in the workshops at the Capel station developed an improved variant of the SSZ, which was first flown in August 1916. The only active attack by one of the Capel airships was carried out on 16 September 1918, when an SSZ depth charged and sunk a German submarine.

It was at Capel that airships first became known as 'blimps'. This apparently described the sound made when the airship's gas bags were plucked to see if they had fully inflated. It is said that this inspired the name of the 1930s satirical cartoon character Colonel Blimp.

RNAS Capel closed in 1919. The site was used as a monitoring station during the Second World War. A permanent monument to the work of the Dover Patrol in the form of a Cleopatra's Needle was erected further along the coast at St Margaret's Bay in 1921.

Abbot's Cliff

Beyond Capel-le-Ferne stands the mighty Abbot's Cliff, over 500 feet high and plunging almost sheer down to the rocks and sea below. A very straight and precipitous path leads down to the foreshore. A good view of the railway line heading off towards Folkestone can be seen from here. Formerly safer than it is now, this rather frightening path was once referred to as the 'goat path', as until the late 1930s goats could be found grazing here, much to the alarm of anyone trying to safely negotiate this narrow track! The goats were perhaps escapees from one of the Warren cottages or the scattered households to be found on the foreshore at the time, of which there is more later.

All along the cliffs from here to Dover and on to St Margaret's Bay are the ruins of old wartime structures; lookout posts, gun emplacements, bunkers and the abandoned Lydden Spout firing range. I can remember as a boy that some friends and I got into many of these old buildings and, armed with torches, we would explore the network of abandoned underground rooms and tunnels left from the Second World War. Nowadays, these have all been conscientiously filled in or obscured so as not to be found, though children and teenagers have a way of finding their way into such dangerous places. Some of the tunnels have now collapsed, I believe. A much safer way to explore this hidden world beneath our feet is via the Underground Kent and Kent Underground Research Group websites.

A Sound Mirror

One of the more striking of these abandoned structures is the sound mirror or 'listening ear' that stands starkly against sea and sky in an exposed position atop Abbot's Cliff. This was put up in 1928, one of a number around the coast. Resembling a megalithic satellite dish, this worked by focusing sound from afar into the centre of its concave dish where an operator could listen through the microphone to distant sounds. In time of war, it was hoped it would be possible to hear enemy aircraft taking off from the French or Belgian coasts. This acoustic aircraft detection system was never used extensively, as radar proved much more effective. The listening equipment has been removed and just the strange concrete structure remains.

The Channel Tunnel and Samphire Hoe

Moving east toward Dover, a large expanse of undercliff becomes visible. This is not a natural formation like Folkestone Warren but entirely man-made. The construction of the railway in 1843 required the blasting away of a large area of the cliff face between Abbot's Cliff and Shakespeare Cliff. The detonation of 18,500 lbs of gunpowder at Round Down on 26 January 1843 was at the time described as the largest man-made explosion in the world, and created a new area of land from the resultant tumbled chalk. This became known as the Great Fall. The railway was then built across the platform of land created.

Sound Mirror at Abbot's Cliff (*Author's photograph*)

Later, in 1880, the first attempt at digging a Channel Tunnel was made near here, but was abandoned just a year later due to security concerns. However, coal was discovered and a coal mine subsequently operated here for a short time from the 1890s until 1915 when it closed, having experienced many difficulties, including one accident that cost the lives of eight miners, and a spectacularly poor productivity record, having only ever brought up 120 tons of coal. The Channel Steel Company took the site over and mined iron ore, but this too closed in the early 1950s.

Another attempt at Channel Tunnel construction took place in 1974/75 but was abandoned on cost grounds. Finally, the dream of a 'Chunnel' became a reality, being given the go ahead in 1986. Construction work was completed in 1993 and the tunnel was officially opened on 6 May 1994. It now carries freight trains, vehicle-carrying shuttle trains and fast Eurostar foot passenger services. Foot passengers board trains at St Pancras, Ebbsfleet or Ashford International stations for journeys to Paris, Lille or Brussels, while vehicles board the shuttle trains at the Eurotunnel terminal at Cheriton, just west of Folkestone, for journeys to a similar terminal in Calais.

During the construction phase of the Chunnel project, access to the tunnel workings on the English side was via the seaside platform created by the railway construction work back in 1843. This platform was extended greatly by the addition of material excavated by the Channel Tunnel workings. This was landscaped and allowed to settle, and become colonised

Previous pages: Old photograph of the 'goat path' in use. (*By kind permission of Kent Libraries and Archives*) and Looking down the 'goat path' and along the railway line to Folkestone, 1995. (*Copyright Ian Pakeman*)

by whatever would naturally take root, and subsequently grazed by cattle and sheep. The new area of land was then managed by the White Cliffs Countryside Project, now known as the White Cliffs Countryside Partnership. A public competition was held to name the new area of land and the winning entry by Gillian Janaway, a retired English teacher from Dover, was the name Samphire Hoe, after the rock samphire that grows on the cliffs here. In 1997, the site was opened to the public as a nature reserve, complete with walking trails, a seawall to be used by anglers, seating, an information and refreshment area and noticeboard displays explaining the natural and human history of the area.

Notable from a natural history point of view are the presence of the early spider orchid, quite a lot of adders, seahorses just offshore, and peregrine falcons nesting in the cliffs above. One of the latter has been measured flying at an astonishing 242 mph!

The Chalk and Channel Way
An unusual and interesting feature to be seen at Samphire Hoe is the wooden Samphire Tower, one of the many artworks along the Chalk and Channel Way, a cycle and footpath between Folkestone and Dover. This was created by Jony Easterby and Pippa Taylor. Inside the tower can be found paintings by Sax Impey and a specially made brass telescope. Elsewhere on the clifftops, there are sculptures by Rob Kesseler in the form of open books, natural history illustrations and much-needed seats. There are also posts where you can listen on your mobile phone to specially commissioned poems by Ros Barber, each one related to the place where you are.

Lydden Spout
Between Samphire Hoe and Abbot's Cliff lies a shingle beach covered at intervals by rockfall debris. This is a wild landscape of massive chalk blocks, sea-built banks of interestingly shaped flints reminiscent of Henry Moore sculptures, and apparent cliff face caves from where clear streams of fresh water emerge. The latter are actually outlets from the Abbot's Cliff railway tunnel. One spring, however, is a strong and pure chalk stream that emerges from the base of the cliffs not far from Samphire Hoe. This is the Lydden Spout spring, clean enough to drink from its source (at your own risk of course) though one should beware of leeches in the water and adders in the surrounding scrub.

Another stream runs into a large debris fan from a massive rock fall in 1911, and creates a pond. The pond water is rather brackish as the sea sometimes spills over the rocks into it. It has a sinister reputation in local lore, for it is said that whenever anyone drowns along this coast, this is where they end up! I don't know how true this is! For this reason, the pond has gained the name Dead Man's Pool.

The rock fall that created this debris fan was notable for another reason. In the early evening of 31 December 1911, such a large amount of chalk fell that it created a wave that minutes later became a 10-foot-high tsunami in the confines of Folkestone Harbour. Luckily there were no casualties, but some fishing boats were damaged and some alarm was felt among local residents, according to newspaper reports of the time.

Among the rock pools near Lydden Spout, and in the chalk marl cliffs above, beautiful, gleaming marcasite nodules and veins of crystals can be found. Don't be misled though: attractive though it is, marcasite has no market value hence it has become known as fool's gold.

Samphire Hoe during construction using spoil from the Channel Tunnel workings, 1993. (*Copyright Ian Pakeman*)

Samphire Hoe today. (*Copyright Candida Wright, 2008*)

Samphire Tower (an artwork on the
Chalk and Channel Way by Jony Easterby
and Pippa Taylor) with the moon above.
(*Copyright Candida Wright, 2008*)

Sculpture by Rob Kesseler.
(*Author's photograph*)

Huts and Homes on the Foreshore

Near the refreshment booth, toilets and car park at Samphire Hoe stand a number of information panels depicting the lives of people who have inhabited this lonely foreshore over the years. Initially, there were cottages for railway workers and miners, but the population soon expanded. The Gatehouse family rented the entire foreshore between Shakespeare and Abbot's Cliffs from the Lord of the Manor at Hougham, a small village just inland. The large Gatehouse family stayed for several generations and added to their cottages on the Great Fall a number of other dwellings, a cabin hut and a boathouse, along the beach towards Lydden Spout. One called simply 'The Cabin' was built in 1919, and was still in use right up to the construction of the Channel Tunnel, but the creation of Samphire Hoe meant it had to go.

Where the Gatehouses led, others followed, some living on the shore all the time, others constructing 'away-from-it-all' huts for seasonal use. An old pumping station serving the Lydden Spout firing range was converted into a holiday home by Ben Tee, and subsequently became known as the Tee Hut. Nearer to Folkestone, another hut was built by Dover coxswain Dave Pascall and used as a retreat for many years. In the early 1980s, there were five such huts on the beach, long after the railway cottages had gone. Eventually, though, stormy seas and cliff falls put paid to all but one of them, which still stands today near the clear Lydden Spout spring.

One family living near Abbot's Cliff became nationally famous in the 1930s for their 'Robinson Crusoe' lifestyle. The Chandlers featured in a Pathé News film called *Robinson Crusoe: Up To Date*, which depicted their apparently jolly, carefree life beneath Abbot's Cliff. In fact, it was anything but. George Chandler had lost his job when his employer went bankrupt in 1928. He had to sell the family home in Dover and move them all into a B&B. Eventually, no longer able to pay the rent, the family were evicted and George cheerfully told his family they were 'going camping'. This camping expedition lasted a full eleven years, during which time the children were educated in their bell tent homes, shopping expeditions were mounted up the cliff paths to Capel-le-Ferne, and the family diet was supplemented with whatever they could forage or fish. The youngest of the Chandlers, Marjorie, was born here and her birth certificate duly gave her place of birth as 'a tent on the foreshore'. The Chandlers were eventually moved away from the shore in 1939 at the outbreak of the Second World War when the coast became out of bounds to the general public.

Recently, this shoreline's hut-building activity seems to have seen a revival, perhaps a sign of hard times. One notable case involves Jeremy Francis, known locally as 'Mungo'. In 2008, Mungo was shipwrecked in his boat *Dolphin* at The Warren following engine trouble. After a year or so of living there, he was moved on by Shepway District Council (SDC) and had his boat towed along the coast to a site beneath Abbot's Cliff, which was outside SDC's area and believed by many to be a 'no man's land' (a map produced by Kent County Council of 'Kent Landscape Information' shows the area between the foreshore and the cliff face as being of unknown ownership). Here, Mungo built a house around his boat, which included plate-glass lounge windows, a veranda, homemade sea defences and a union flag fluttering from a flagpole. Like the Chandlers, Mungo made a minor cinematic debut. A documentary film called *Life's a Beach* was made about him and had its premiere at the Quarterhouse in Folkestone on 10 April 2012, where it was warmly received by a packed audience. The film screening raised £1,250 for the Royal National Lifeboat Institution (RNLI). Sadly, Mungo died the previous year following a cycling accident.

The story of the lives of some of the people living under the cliffs here is told in a fascinating book called *Shakespeare Cliff: A People's History*, which was published by Dover District Council (DDC) and the White Cliffs Countryside Project (WCCP) in 2008. The book and the oral history project from which it resulted were both part of a Local Heritage Initiative funded by the Heritage Lottery Fund and the Nationwide Building Society.

Successor to the Tee Hut, 1981. (*Author's photograph*)

Dave Pascall's hut, 1981. (*Author's photograph*)

Mungo in the beached *Dolphin* in 2008. (*Author's photograph*)

Mungo's house beneath Abbot's Cliff in 2011. (*Author's photograph*)

Shakespeare Cliff with Dover beyond, 1986. (*Author's photograph*)

Shakespeare Cliff

Our final point of interest before reaching Dover is the distinctively angled Shakespeare Cliff. The name derives from the assumption at some point in the past that this was the spot William Shakespeare had in mind in Act VI, Scene VII (The Country near Dover) of his play *King Lear*. In this we read:

> How fearful
> And dizzy 'tis to cast one's eyes so low-
> The crows and the choughs that wing midway
> air show scarce so gross as beetles,
> halfway down
> Hangs one that gathers samphire-
> dreadful trade!

Samphire gatherers would indeed have frequented these cliffs, but whether it was this particular one, if any, that Shakespeare was thinking of, we will never know. As it is, this is probably not as fearful as some of the cliffs encountered earlier, such as Abbot's Cliff that I certainly won't go near the edge of!

By the time we reach Shakespeare Cliff, their height is declining. On the approach to Dover, we have dropped 200 feet since Abbot's Cliff to a mere 300 feet above sea level. From Shakespeare Cliff, Dover can be glimpsed with its large and busy harbour, its impressive castle and the sheer white cliffs beyond.

5

Around Dover

From Shakespeare Cliff, the town of Dover opens up in front of us. The Western Docks lay seaward and the green hills beyond the ever busy A20 lie inland. Various block like structures can be seen on these hills, known as the Western Heights. These are historically important Napoleonic fortifications, the largest in Britain. They were later used in the First and Second World Wars and are now largely abandoned. They form part of a local nature reserve run by the White Cliffs Countryside Partnership (WCCP). The area is an important example of chalk grassland with way-marked trails from which, in the summer months, several types of orchid and butterflies in profusion can be seen; the Chalkhill Blue and Marbled White are particularly notable. Kestrels hover over the hills, while Dexter cattle and Konik ponies graze below.

The old fortifications are brought to life at regular intervals by a local re-enactment group. An impressive triple spiral staircase links the top with the base of the cliffs, built to allow quick access to the shore by troops from the barracks above. The staircase, known as the Grand Shaft, is run by the Western Heights Preservation Society and is open some weekends and on special open days.

The Western Docks – Hovercraft and Cruise Ships

The Western Docks is one half of Dover's vast dock area, the other half being at other end of an attractive seafront promenade and known, unsurprisingly, as the Eastern Docks. At the western end there was once a hoverport. The first cross-Channel hovercraft flight came up onto the beach near here on 25 July 1959. The SRN1, as it was known (the manufacturers being Saunders-Roe and the 'N' standing for 'nautical'), was succeeded by more advanced models and culminated in the SRN4, which was rolled out in 1967 and entered service on the Dover-Calais route on 31 July 1968, and the Dover–Boulogne route the following day. SRN4 was capable of carrying 254 passengers and 30 cars across the Channel in about 30 minutes. Ten years later, the SRN4s were stretched to increase passenger and vehicle capacity to 418 and 60 respectively.

However, the hovercraft, fast and impressive as they were, did suffer from a number of drawbacks: they were very noisy, expensive to run and difficult to operate in rough weather. The final SRN4 hovercraft crossing by the *Princess Anne* took place on 1 October 2000, after which they retired after thirty-three years of service. Catamaran and jetfoil services also ran from Western Docks, but both have now ceased operation.

A rail line formerly serviced the docks here, terminating at the Dover Marine Station. When this station was closed, the area was redeveloped into an important cruise ship terminal, second only to Southampton. The first terminal opened in 1993, with a second added in 2000. Regular arrivals of some very impressive, large cruise liners can be seen from the terminal, many carrying over 2,000 passengers. A number of important lines use this as their principal port of departure. The largest cruise liner seen in Dover at the time of writing has been the 112,000-ton *Carnival Splendor*, which came to Dover for her naming ceremony in 2008.

Pictured above is a Marbled White and below is a Chalkhill Blue. (*Paul Sampson, WCCP*)

From Shakespeare Cliff, a view across the Western and Eastern Docks to the cliffs. (*Author's photograph*)

SRN4 hovercraft in action. (*Copyright Ian Pakeman, 1999*)

Crest of a Wave sculpture by Ray Smith, marking the beginning or end of the Chalk and Channel Way walking and cycle route on the Dover seafront promenade. (*Author's photograph*)

Seafront Promenade

The promenade linking the two ends of Dover's vast harbour area is of much interest in itself. A new sea sports centre opened in 2010, providing nautical activity of a more modest kind in the large enclosed harbour area. Just inland is a marina and shopping complex from which boat trips can be taken around the harbour, or, more ambitiously, east and north along the base of the cliffs, and out to the common and grey seal colonies at either the Goodwin Sands off Deal or the estuary of the River Stour near Sandwich, 15 miles away. The beginning or end of the previously mentioned walking and cycle route known as the Chalk and Channel Way is marked on the promenade by the monolithic *Crest of a Wave* sculpture by Ray Smith.

Channel Crossings

The Dover seafront promenade exhibits several statues celebrating notable Channel crossings. One is of Charles Stewart Rolls, the first man to fly the Channel both ways in a single flight back in 1910. The first ever cross-Channel flight by heavier than air aircraft was, of course, completed the previous year by Louis Blériot, and a monument in the shape of an aircraft can be found in the grass of a field behind Dover Castle. Blériot was himself pre-dated by Jean-Pierre Blanchard, who made the first ever cross-Channel flight from Dover to Calais by balloon in 1785.

There is also a statue of Matthew Webb, who became the first person to swim the Channel back in 1875 and started an ongoing tradition that continues to this day. Channel swimmers can often be seen practicing in Dover Harbour or at the East Cliff Sands at Folkestone. Most of the actual Channel swimming attempts, however, set off from St Margaret's Bay, 3 miles to the north of here, that being the nearest point to France.

Dover seafront promenade. (*Author's photograph*)

At the eastern end of the promenade is a plaque in memory of the fifty-eight Chinese people who died of asphyxiation in the back of a lorry while attempting to illegally enter the country at the Eastern Docks in June 2000, the victims of people trafficking.

The Eastern Docks

The Eastern Docks are currently the hub of the cross-Channel ferry business, through which some 16 million passengers pass every year. In fact, it is the busiest ferry port in Europe. Some of the boats operating from here are truly huge, with some of cruiseliner size and resembling floating shopping centres complete with car and lorry parks. For instance, the 25,000-ton *Stena Fantasia* holds 1,800 passengers and 650 cars or 120 lorries, while the *Seafrance Berlioz* carries 1,900 passengers and 700 cars or 120 lorries. Safety and comfort are much improved since 1987 when on 6 March, the Townsend Thoresen *Herald of Free Enterprise* capsized off Zeebrugge in Belgium, with the loss of 193 lives. This was a disaster that affected the whole community of Dover and nearby towns. Nearly everyone working at the docks or living in the town was either directly affected by this terrible accident or knew someone who was. A window commemorating this tragic event can be seen at St Mary's church in Dover town centre.

Historic Dover

Bronze Age Boat and Roman Hotel

Dover is not only about docks and Channel crossings, it is also an immensely interesting historic town in its own right. The excellent museum in Market Square documents this well and has a special gallery displaying the remains of a Bronze Age seagoing boat. This was

IN MEMORY OF
58
YOUNG PEOPLE FROM CHINA
WHO DIED NEAR HERE
ON
18TH JUNE 2000
ALL HUMAN LIFE IS PRECIOUS

所有人的生命都 是宝贵的
纪念在2000 年6月18日
在此去逝 的58位 中国青年

Plaque in memory of fifty-eight Chinese people who died in the back of a lorry attempting to enter the UK through Dover. (*Author's photograph*)

discovered in 1992 at Langdon Bay, east of the town, where it had sunk approximately 3,550 years before, carrying a cargo of some 350 axes, daggers, chisels and other tools, many in bronze. A seven-year conservation effort by the Dover Bronze Age Boat Trust has resulted in the preservation and display of this, the world's oldest seagoing vessel, in the impressive state of the art Bronze Age Boat Gallery. A half-size replica of the boat was constructed and rowed around Dover Harbour successfully (that is it didn't sink) on 7 September 2013.

Next to the museum is another notable piece of preserved history from the Roman period. Known as the Roman Painted House and billed as 'Britain's Buried Pompeii', this is a fine example of a Roman house, complete with mosaics and underfloor heating, discovered by the Kent Archaeological Rescue Unit in 1970. The house was built around AD 200 as an official hotel for traders crossing the Channel, and was later partially demolished and covered over to make way for a fort around AD 270. This infilling is the cause of its preservation.

Dover Castle, 'The Key to England'

Most impressive of all Dover's historical attractions, and a world-class feature, along with the Bronze Age Boat and Roman Painted House, is the twelfth-century Dover Castle, once known as the 'key to England', that dominates the town from its lofty site upon East Cliff or Castle Cliff. Here this mighty medieval edifice looms beckoningly atop the resumption of the White Cliffs east of Dover. Although there was a first-century Roman lighthouse or 'pharos' and a Romano-British and later Saxon church here (now St Mary's in Castro), both of which can still be visited, the castle as we see it today is largely down to Henry II, who instituted the construction of these huge fortifications on the site of earlier Norman earthworks.

Left: Window commemorating the *Herald of Free Enterprise* tragedy. (*Author's photograph*)

Below: Remains of the Bronze Age boat displayed in Dover Museum. (*By kind permission of Dover Museum*)

Views of Dover Castle, one of the largest fortifications in medieval Europe. (*Author's photographs*)

At the time of its construction in the twelfth century, Dover Castle was not only the greatest medieval fortress in England, but in the whole of Western Europe, as well as the first concentric medieval fortification. The castle currently displays its history in most spectacular fashion. the Keep or Great Tower, built in the 1170s to 1780s illustrates how its many rooms were not the empty, grey-stone chambers generally imagined, but colourful, luxurious apartments, truly fit for a magnificent king. The King's Hall is dominated by a canopied throne, decked with wall hangings and housing recreations of contemporary furniture. Costumed actors playing the parts of Henry II, his queen and family, hold court in some of the rooms and wander The Keep and surrounding grounds, telling their stories to the many thousands of visitors from all over the world who explore this medieval wonder almost every day of the year. If you like castles, they don't come any better than this!

The Siege of Dover Castle, 1216

Dover Castle's history did not stop in the reign of Henry II. In 1216, during the civil war between King John and the barons, the castle came under siege. A French force under Prince Louis Capet landed in Thanet in May 1216 in support of the barons who aimed to put Louis on the throne. King John provided Dover Castle with 140 knights under Hubert de Burgh, Justiciar of England, to await siege by the French forces.

Based at Dover Priory, with his main encampment on high ground north of the castle, Louis directed the siege against what was considered to be the 'key to England'. Stone-throwing engines or trebuchets were used to bombard the outer walls, while miners were sent to tunnel beneath the northern barbican and the eastern of the two gate towers that were subsequently brought crashing to the ground. The castle had sent out frequent raids on the siege army and countermines were dug to cut off the French miners, but to no avail. When the gate tower collapsed, French soldiers poured into the castle to face Hubert de Burgh's knights. De Burgh's forces fought back valiantly and repulsed the invaders, though the siege continued inconclusively for a while until a truce was called in the autumn of 1216. Shortly after, King John died of dysentery and was succeeded by Henry III. In May 1217, the truce was broken and the siege of Dover Castle resumed for a few days until the French were soundly defeated at Lincoln and the siege was finally lifted. An attempted resupply of French forces in August of that year was intercepted off Sandwich and after a fierce sea battle, English sailors won the day and the civil war came to an end.

Dover Castle continued in a defensive role right up to modern times. An interesting artefact from the Elizabethan era is the huge wheel-mounted gun of Dutch origin that dominates the restaurant. This was made in 1544 and presented to Henry VIII by Emperor Charles V from the people of Holland in gratitude for British help against Spain. This was installed at Dover Castle in 1613 and became known as Queen Elizabeth's Pocket Pistol.

Operation Dynamo

In 1797, a network of tunnels were dug under the castle as part of defensive measures against an expected French invasion. These were reoccupied during the Second World War and became the nerve centre for Operation Dynamo, the rescue of British and Allied troops from the beach at Dunkirk, run from here by Vice Admiral Bertram Ramsay.

In May 1940, Operation Dynamo organised and directed the successful evacuation of some 338,000 members of the British and French armies by mobilising an armada of small boats and ships that sailed to France and endured intense German fire to carry out their brave mission. This was another of the heroic episodes of Dover's history, echoing the earlier corralling of 'little ships' for the Dover Patrol during the First World War. The underground tunnels also contained an underground hospital and nurses' dormitories. Today these tunnels are open to the public, and give a well-presented impression of what life was like here in the tunnels and in the town of Dover when the area was under intense Nazi bombardment and known as 'Hellfire Corner'.

Cold War Role

After the war, Dover Castle remained an Army garrison until 1958 and was opened to the public in 1962. However, in that year the Cuban Missile Crisis brought the world to the brink of nuclear war. The British government decided to set up a series of underground Regional Seats of Government (RSG) from where the country would be run in the aftermath of a nuclear attack. Dover Castle was one of the sites selected and would have governed Kent, Sussex and Surrey. The RSG contained radiation-proof living accommodation for hundreds of government workers and landline communication links with other local and central government agencies. The RSG was abandoned in 1984 and taken off the secret list.

Today Dover Castle is run by English Heritage who, since 1990, have opened up the underground tunnels, principally depicting life here during the Second World War when Dover came under intense bombardment from both air raids and shelling from across the Channel. Some of the RSG is also recreated, though to see a complete example of one of these, a visit to the Secret Nuclear Bunker at Kelvedon Hatch, near Brentwood in Essex, is recommended.

The Ghosts of Dover Castle

Before we leave Dover Castle, let's take a look at the ghost stories that have arisen here over the last twenty-five years or so. Before 1990, few ghost reports were made by visitors to the castle. There were long standing legends of a Napoleonic period 'headless drummer boy', a ghostly cavalier and a spectral seventeenth-century pikeman seen in the Keep, but these seem little more than folklore. In fact, Peter Underwood in his 1980 book *Ghosts of Kent*, remarks on Dover Castle's lack of 'good ghosts'.

That didn't stop the Thanet Paranormal Research Group conducting all-night vigils in the Keep during October and November 1991. A number of teams were located at different sites around the Keep, equipped with various sensors, tape recorders and, in some places, video recorders.

During the first nightwatch, sounds like heavy wooden doors slamming shut were heard at various places and recorded on tape. Researcher Ian Peters of the Association for the Scientific Study of Anomalous Phenomena (ASSAP) said he was enveloped in an 'enormous sound' that he could not describe, followed by a small 'ping' when the sound stopped. Most unnerving of all was the violent shaking of two large double doors that left 'ghost hunters' Maria and Adrian Coombs-Hoar 'petrified'. Nevertheless, they did investigate the shaking, which stopped when they approached the doors. Unlocking them, Adrian Coombs-Hoar could find no obvious explanation of the mystery. Four hours later, in the same room, University of Kent philosophy teacher Chris Cherry also witnessed the same doors shaking violently and deliberately, while flags suspended from the walls fluttered overhead. The video recording of the event, which I have seen, leaves me in no doubt that the doors were deliberately shaken rather than blown by the wind, which was admittedly strong that night. Had someone been having fun at the researchers' expense? From another vantage point, one team member who heard the doors 'vibrating' also heard what sounded to him like a dustbin rolling down the stairs that lay at the other side of the doors. Someone making a quick getaway, perhaps? An ITV television programme called *Strange but True?* was made about these events and screened in 1991.

Down in the underground tunnels, known as 'Hellfire Corner' for tourism purposes, ghostly incidents have often been reported. The first incident took place in the Defence Telecommunications Repeater Station, where a female tourist collapsed after a supposedly spectral encounter. Upon enquiry by tour guide Leslie Simpson, the woman explained that she had seen a man in naval uniform walk towards and 'through' her, upon which she collapsed. A couple of years later another guide, Karen Mennie, noticed a man in conversation with an unseen figure. When the tunnel's ghost stories were mentioned by the guide, the tourist told Karen that he had just spoken to the ghost! He said the 'ghost' had explained he was a postal telecommunications officer from Canterbury called Bill Billings, who was killed while assembling one of the amplifier racks. These and other similar sightings and encounters were reported as factual experiences at the time, but I must admit to being a little sceptical.

Dover Castle is an extremely atmospheric place and people do have fun with ghost stories, but imagination and storytelling apart, I can't help noticing that costumed actors portraying past residents of the castle now routinely converse with visitors, holograms are projected and ghost tours run, all part of the varied entertainment provided by English Heritage. Perhaps this was all in an experimental stage back in the 1990s? To enquire further might spoil the fun, so let us move on.

The Cave Dwellers of Dover

Beyond Dover Castle, the cliffs take on a rather artificial appearance. This is the result of late nineteenth-century work creating the Eastern Docks. The green shelf running along the cliff face was the route of a former railway used during the construction of the docks below, and for conveying materials for road building up from the docks to Martin Mill station. This railway closed in 1937, but was reused as a base for track-mounted guns in the Second World War. The development of the harbour and linked rail line obliterated a particularly interesting aspect of Dover's past, that of its one-time troglodytes.

My attention was first drawn to this fascinating piece of local history by Louisa Burville, whose father, Dr Peter Burville, was researching a book on the former cave dwellers of the Dover cliffs, some of whom were his ancestors. The book, *The White Cliffs of Dover: Images of Cliff and Shore* by Peter and Julie Burville, was published in 2001 and revised in 2003. It illustrates, using highly magnified images from detail on very early (mid-nineteenth-century) plate photographs of the chalk cliffs east of Dover, various caves, paths, steps, fences and other evidence of these former dwellings that apparently existed on an undercliff ledge, originally created, it is thought, by a major earthquake in 1580. Some fine detail blown up from these magnifications even appear to show people going about their business or chatting with neighbours outside their caves. The original photographs are currently stored in the archives of Dover Museum.

Peter Burville's ancestor, Mary Burville, seems to have been here from at least 1833, as she is named in a report in the *Dover Telegraph*, which describes the death of her husband after falling from a cart. She is described as 'living in a cavern'.

Paintings by W. H. Prior dated to between 1833 and 1857 are reproduced in the Burville's book. These show an East Cliff cave cottage from the outside in one painting and an interior view in another. The interior consists of rooms, shelves, cupboards, recesses and windows, all carved out of the chalk. The Burville's remark on the convenience of this type of dwelling, in that a new room, cubby hole or shelf could be carved when required at no expense other than the labour involved.

In Peter Burvilles subsequent book, *An East Kent Family: The Burvilles*, he tells how the 1841 census shows charwoman Mary Burville living with her four children 'under the cliff'.

East Cliff Cave Cottage, painting by W. H. Prior, *c.* 1833–57. (*By kind permission of Dover Museum*)

East Cliff Cave Cottage Interior, painting by W. H. Prior, *c.* 1833–57. (*By kind permission of Dover Museum*)

The Tithe Map and Return Schedule of 1843 records that Mary occupied a 'cottage in a cliff'. The Tithe Map shows this property near the foot of the cliff just east of where the Jubilee Way flyover now takes heavy lorries from the docks up to the A2, the main road to London. The 1851 census shows widow Mary as a laundress living at East Cliff in a cave with her two daughters and two sons. By the 1860s, however, the Burvilles had moved into more conventional accommodation in Dover. A painting by Samuel Gillespie Prout dating to the 1860s shows one of the cave cottages in a rather decayed condition. The cave cottages were finally obliterated by the construction of Admiralty Harbour at the end of the nineteenth century.

Elsewhere along the cliffs between Folkestone and Kingsdown there are still caves and tunnels in existence today. These are mostly of artificial construction, many from the Second World War. As a teenager, I, along with others of my age, explored some of these. Today most of the caves and tunnels have had their entrances filled in, though some are accessible if you know where to look. Naturally, I would not recommend exploration from the point of view of safety, but there are those that do and details of their explorations can be found on the websites dealing with 'Underground Kent'.

Langdon Cliffs

Above the site of the former cave cottages there is now a car parking area with a National Trust Visitor Centre, which is a retail and refreshment stop, and excellent views over the busy comings and goings of ferries and other vessels in and out of the Eastern Docks. There are also fine walks along the cliffs towards South Foreland and its lighthouse, St Margaret's Bay, and for the more adventurous, onward to Kingsdown, Walmer and Deal.

The two large communication masts that dominate the scene just inland were once four, and an early radar installation during the Second World War. In the 1950s, the masts changed appearance and reduced to three, with a pyramidal structure constructed at their base in the late 1970s as part of a Cold War early warning system. Now there are just two masts and the radar dishes have been taken away. Whether they still have a role, and if so, just what that might be, I cannot say.

From here, the remainder of the cliffs (another 6 miles) are largely owned by the National Trust, having been acquired in stages over recent decades. A series of clifftop stretches are signposted along the way: Langdon Cliffs, Langdon Hole, The Leas, Bockhill Farm and Kingsdown Leas. From Langdon Cliffs we pass into the area known as South Foreland, and onto our next chapter.

Gateway sign to the White Cliffs, owned by the National Trust. (*Author's photograph*)

Cave Cottage painting by Samuel Gillespie Prout. (*By kind permission of Dr Peter Burville*)

View over the busy Eastern Docks (*Author's photograph*)

View back towards Dover from Langdon Cliffs across docks to Shakespeare Cliff. (*Author's photograph*)

Previous page: A typical cave in the White Cliffs. (*Author's photograph*)

White Cliffs of Dover (South Foreland)
painting, by Diana Harrison. (*Reproduced
by kind permission of Diana Harrison*)

Cliffs above Fan Bay. (*Author's
photograph*)

6

South Foreland to St Margaret's Bay

From Langdon Cliffs to Kingsdown is, for the walker, perhaps the most pleasant stretch of the White Cliffs. Here you will find open downland, gently undulating atop gleaming white, sheer cliffs that drop straight down to the rocky shore below. These are the classic white cliffs of the famous wartime Vera Lynn song. Exmoor ponies wander amiably about, while skylarks (not bluebirds) twitter overhead. The rich National Trust-managed grassland is alive with bees and butterflies during the summer months, including the rare Chalk Hill Blue. The landscape seems devoid of litter, while the straight, level footpaths allow a good couple of hours of fine walking. In August 2013, the National Trust published a list of their 'top ten' lesser-known or 'secret' recommended walks. The White Cliffs of Dover was in the number one position. I was walking the walk just two days later and I think I can safely say it's not a secret anymore!

Shipwrecks

With the coastguard station at your back, the view eastward takes in Langdon Hole with an impressive 400-foot cliff beyond. A steep footpath and vertical ladder can take the intrepid walker to the shore, although at the time of writing this is unusable due to a recent rock fall. Here, at low tide, can be seen the remains of a shipwreck. This is all that is left of the steamer *Falcon* that caught fire and drifted ashore while on passage from Ostend to London in October 1926. Some 3,500 years earlier, the world's oldest known seagoing boat came to grief here and, as earlier described, can now be seen excellently preserved and presented in Dover Museum.

A mile or so further on at Fan Hole, another dip in the downland is overlooked by another striking, white, vertical cliff. Here, a major wreck occurred. One of the largest vessels of her day, the German five-masted sailing vessel *Preussen*, was wrecked following a collision with the Newhaven–Dieppe steamer *Brighton* on 6 November 1910, and forced to return up Channel due to bow damage. She then lost both anchors off Dungeness and drifted helplessly ashore here at Fan Bay. At low tide, the ribs and bottom plates become visible on the rocky shore.

Ahead, beyond Fan Hole, the white 'pepperpot' of South Foreland Lighthouse comes into view. The fields on these clifftops were the scene of another of the many unusual Channel crossings that have been made over the years, some of which we have already looked at. On 28 September 2008, forty-nine-year-old Yves Rossy flew across the Channel by jetpack. Rossy, wearing a fireproof suit and with a pack of four kerosene-fuelled Jet Cat model aircraft engines strapped to his back, jumped from a plane 8,200 feet above Calais, and was propelled in just thirteen minutes to a parachute landing in a field near the South Foreland Lighthouse.

Above left: Langdon Hole from Langdon Cliffs. (*Photograph by Candida Wright*). *Above right*: Cliffs above Fan Bay. (*Author's photograph*)

South Foreland Lighthouse

It is claimed that the first lighthouse here was a light left burning in a cave from 1367 by the hermit monk Nicholas de Legh to warn mariners of the proximity of the dangerous shore. Later, in 1859, Thomas Edison first tried out an electric light for the purpose at the South Foreland Lighthouse. Michael Faraday also worked on electricity here, and Gugliemo Marconi carried out his first successful ship-to-shore radio experiments here on 24 December 1898, and the first radio transmissions across the Channel the following year. A notable feature of the present lighthouse is that it is the highest lighthouse in the country (being situated on a 300-foot-high cliff), and that it is the first place in Britain to catch the summer sunrise on New Year's Day. A locally produced tourist information leaflet consequently calls this immediate area 'First Light Coast and Country' as part of its promotion to visitors. The current lighthouse once worked in conjunction with an earlier one that now stands on private land near the cliff edge. The modern lighthouse was manned until automated in 1969, and was finally made redundant in 1988. Today it is owned by the National Trust and open to the public. Guided tours are run most summer afternoons.

St Margaret's Bay

This beautiful little bay can be approached by foot along the coastal path from either direction, or by road following the signs from the main Dover to Deal road, passing through

Cliffs above Fan Bay. (*Author's photograph*)

the village of St Margaret's at Cliffe, and taking a narrow, winding route down between the cliffs to the sheltered seashore cove. For the purposes of this book, I approached by foot from Dover. There is a choice of approach, staying nearer the cliff edge or descending through the South Foreland Valley, which is more sheltered. Both end up at exactly the same place. The South Foreland Valley is another nature reserve managed by WCCP. This area, like so many in the Kent Downs, was once open grassland but has been increasingly overrun by bushes and trees. Downland still exists in small pockets, though, and basil thyme can be found here, as well as many butterfly species. To increase the amount of downland habitat, grazing is being reintroduced using both Konik ponies and Dexter cattle.

St Margaret's Bay is the nearest point on our coast to France, which is only 21 miles from this point. Consequently, it has become the traditional starting and finishing place for many a Channel swimming attempt.

The Pines Garden and Calyx

The bay has a warm microclimate, being south facing with cliffs either side and behind that shelter it from north, east and westerly winds. This is evidenced by the subtropical nature of many of the gardens here. A beautiful area of public gardens near the shore called The Pines is well worth exploring. This contains a wealth of interesting plants, a grass labyrinth, cascade and adjoining lake, and a 9-foot-high bronze statue of Sir Winston Churchill, created by sculptor Oscar Nemon in 1972. There is also a remarkable, rotund building in the

Left: Old lighthouse near the cliff edge.

Below: Tiny figures stand near the edge of vertical cliffs at South Foreland. (*Author's photograph*)

South Foreland Lighthouse.
(*Author's photographs*)

gardens known as the Calyx. This is a conference and events venue, which hosts workshops, training courses and seminars, and can also be hired out for weddings. The Calyx is built of chalk from the surrounding landscape, and is said to have the lowest carbon footprint of any commercial building in the United Kingdom. It has been granted no fewer than eight national and international design awards. The Calyx catering team use over forty different species of fruit and vegetables, all grown in the Pines Gardens.

Opposite these fine gardens is a small museum of local history, including another known as Hellfire Corner, which explains and illustrates both local life during the Second World War and the lives of one-time celebrity residents Sir Noël Coward and Ian Fleming.

Sir Noël Coward, actor, composer and playwright, acted in his first play at the age of twelve and produced his first play *The Vortex* in 1924 at the age of twenty-five. This was followed by the popular comedy *Hay Fever* in 1925, and his most popular musical *Bitter Sweet* in 1929. Perhaps Coward's best known film was the classic *Brief Encounter*, which is still highly regarded today. I remember him for *Blithe Spirit*, a play that was produced as an entertaining film in the 1950s starring Rex Harrison and set in the countryside near Folkestone.

In the early 1950s, Coward lived in a house under the cliffs of St Margaret's Bay, which he called White Cliffs Cottage. However, he soon found the area becoming too popular with visitors for his liking and sold the house to his friend Ian Fleming, who, of course, is best known as the author of the James Bond novels.

James Bond in Kent

Ian Fleming drew on his knowledge of the Kent countryside that he loved in some of his James Bond novels. Several chapters of *Goldfinger* are set around Reculver, Ramsgate and Sandwich, while almost all of *Moonraker* takes place in Kent, much of it on the coast between Dover and Deal.

For those that don't know, *Moonraker*, published in 1955, concerns mega-rich entrepreneur Hugo Drax, who builds, on contract to the British government, a ballistic missile system to defend the United Kingdom. This is all a cover for a dastardly scheme by Drax (who turns out to be a Nazi bent on revenge) to use a test launch of the rocket, from a base on the cliffs near Kingsdown, to drop a nuclear bomb on London. As you might expect, the scheme is thwarted in the nick of time by James Bond and undercover agent Gala Brand, who change the coordinates of the rocket's guidance system, leading to its veering off course and landing in the North Sea where the warhead explodes destroying ships in the vicinity, including a Russian submarine containing Hugo Drax. The story is well told, moves at a satisfying pace and is based more on fact than might be supposed.

For instance, 007 (this number, by the way, is reliably said to have been inspired by the National Express Dover to London via Canterbury coach, which is numbered 007) is told by his boss 'M' to investigate 'an RAF establishment ... part of the big radar network along the east coast about 3 miles north of Dover'. Although Fleming bases this facility at Kingsdown, he seems to have in mind a radar installation on the cliffs above his house in St Margaret's Bay.

An early 1950s postcard view of St Margaret's Bay shows Ian Fleming's White Cliffs Cottage at the foot of the cliffs, with radar dishes along the top. Originally set up in the Second World War, this station was involved in trying to divert incoming V2 missiles heading for London, just as James Bond and Gala Brand did to the *Moonraker* rocket in the novel. The radar station became a Cold War ROTOR station with a huge nuclear bombproof underground bunker in the early 1950s. The entrance to the underground complex was through an innocuous-looking bungalow on the clifftop. A good example of a ROTOR station, complete with façade bungalow entrance, that later became a Regional Seat of Government, can be seen at Kelvedon Hatch near Brentwood in Essex. This is now open to the public as a tourist attraction.

Views of St Margaret's Bay and its surrounding cliffs. (*Author's photographs*)

The Calyx with sea views from the Pines Garden.

Nearby on the clifftop can be seen a Cleopatra's Needle-type obelisk, erected in 1921 to commemorate the work of the Dover Patrol during the First World War. Perhaps this suggested the idea of the *Moonraker* rocket in this vicinity to Fleming.

There is, however, a more substantial background to *Moonraker* than just ideas inspired by local features. Some of this was revealed by Sean Longden in his 2009 book *T Force: The Race for Nazi War Secrets, 1945*, and Nicholas Rankin in *Ian Fleming's Commandos: The Story of 30 Assault Unit in WWII*, published in 2011. Target Force, or 'T Force', was created in 1944 to capture key personnel and technology from German forces. The concept of T Force was based on the success of 30 Assault Unit, which had been created at the suggestion of none other than Naval Intelligence Officer Ian Fleming for a similar purpose. Targets such as key German technical personnel, plans, remaining technology and workshops were selected for the attention of T Force by, among others, Ian Fleming.

In May 1945, T Force seized the port of Kiel and a research centre where engines for German rockets and missiles were designed. Soon afterwards, British forces commenced Operation Backfire, which used German scientists and technicians to build new V2s from the captured parts. These were then launched from a site near the German town of Cuxhaven for research purposes.

Old postcard view showing ROTOR radars and the Dover Patrol monument above Ian Fleming's house in St Margaret's Bay. (*Photographer unknown*)

A Blue Streak rocket on display at the
National Space Centre, Leicester, 2001.
(*Author's photograph*)

Dover Patrol monument, St Margaret's Bay.
(*Photograph by Candida Wright*)

Kingsdown Cliffs. (*Author's photograph*)

One of the captured German scientists brought back to Britain, where he assembled a team of specialist scientists and engineers, was a Dr Hellmuth Walter, Germany's foremost expert in hydrogen peroxide rocket propulsion. In *Moonraker*, Hugo Drax's leading scientist, who was running his rocket programme, is named as none other than Dr Walter, also an expert in hydrogen peroxide rocket propulsion!

The real Dr Walter had developed a rocket plane for the Nazis known as the ME163 that could take a pilot up to 30,000 feet in two and a half minutes, and fly for five minutes before gliding back down to a runway landing. His ideas were incorporated into the RAF's early delta-winged jet fighters such as the Swallow, the Vixen and the Venom. The de Havilland DH106 Comet, the world's first commercial passenger jet airliner, which first flew with the British Overseas Aircraft Corporation (BOAC) in 1949, was derived from Dr Hellmuth Walter's research. The Comet later became the long-running Nimrod early warning spy plane that was finally phased out in 2010.

More factual elements in the *Moonraker* story relate to the rocket itself. This was based on Blue Streak, a medium-range ballistic missile project commenced in 1954, when Fleming was writing his book. Blue Streak was due to be launched from silos in southern England but was abandoned as a missile project in 1960, eventually being replaced by submarine-based nuclear missile systems such as Polaris, and more recently Trident. Some of the technology for Blue Streak was developed using a rocket called Black Knight.

The launch programme for Black Knight started in 1958 and took place from Woomera, Australia. Test firings of the Saunders-Roe engines for Black Knight were, however, carried out on the white cliffs of southern England, though not near Dover, but above the Needles on the Isle of Wight. Some of these preceded the launch programme and although not public knowledge at the time, they, or at least the plans for them, were probably known about by Ian Fleming. He of course translocated their fictional equivalent to the cliffs between St Margaret's Bay and Kingsdown.

A James Bond film called *Moonraker* was released in 1979, though it bore little resemblance to the original novel. A leaflet about this area's connections with James Bond called 'James Bond Country' is available from local tourist information centres, though may be out of print at the time of writing.

The Leas

Leaving behind St Margaret's Bay and its rather exotic atmosphere, a stepped path takes us up on to a clifftop of down and scrub, another stretch of coastline owned by the National Trust, known as The Leas. Leas just means fields but seems to be used as a name for grassy clifftop areas, i.e. The Leas at Folkestone or Kingsdown Leas, a mile and a half north of here. Here you will find Exmoor ponies grazing (some of the time), an old coastguard station now a café, and the impressive Dover Patrol monument mentioned previously. The view from here along the coast turns north towards Kingsdown and Walmer, our next and final ports of call.

7

Kingsdown and Walmer

The View North

As the coastline of the White Cliffs turns north, there is a subtle change of atmosphere. The prevailing wind generally comes now from across the land rather than the sea, bearing with it scents from the fertile fields of the Kent Downs, rather than a salty breeze from down Channel. The air seems different, calmer. The sea to your right is starting to change from the Channel to the North Sea. The view ahead takes the eye across the rolling downs, descending to the Stour Estuary and the Isle of Thanet, visible as a distant line of gleaming cliffs. Beyond this, a large number of mysterious white spires can be seen. Actually there are a hundred or so of these, and on clear days or through binoculars they resolve themselves into windmills, in fact the largest offshore wind farm in the world, miles away in the Thames Estuary. To the east, the Goodwin Sands are sometimes made visible at low tide by the waves breaking against them, and to the west, shrub-covered barrows, the final resting place of some long-forgotten chieftains of the Bronze Age Beaker folk, march across this ancient landscape on a supposed ley line to the sea.

This area, known as Bockhill Farm, was acquired by the National Trust in 1974, and along with the more recently purchased Kingsdown Leas beyond it, form perhaps the finest stretch of walking along this coast: it is quiet, apart from the occasional gull, lush and fertile, particularly in summer, litter-free and again with straight, levelled paths paralleling the ever changing sea. The cliffs here are slightly lower in altitude than previously, at only about 200 feet, but now sheer, white walls plunge vertically to the sea. One hesitates to look over the edge, the magnetic pull of vertigo an ever present danger.

There are 2 miles of superb walking and then the footpath descends to sea level. Below the cliffs here is an old Royal Marines firing range, now abandoned, forming a sort of scrubby undercliff through which a footpath leads to a secluded beach, sometimes favoured by naturist bathers. In *Moonraker*, James Bond and Gala Brand walked from here to St Margaret's Bay, went swimming on this beach and were nearly buried alive by a rock fall engineered by Hugo Drax. The 007 Magazine website calls this bit of coast the 'Moonraker Cliffs'.

From here the footpath undulates across the remainder of the cliffs as they descend in altitude, 100 feet, 50 feet, then, just before Walmer Castle, down to nothing, to sea level.

From these final cliffs, Walmer, Deal, with its pier, and the Isle of Thanet beckon. Kingsdown is a cluster of houses and cottages spilling down an old valley to the seashore. Here on the shore in front of the welcoming Zetland Arms public house, a line of beach huts sit on the shingle beach. This beach incidentally is where Gertrude Ederle, on 6 August 1926, ended her epic 35-mile swim in 14 hours and 39 minutes, to become the first woman the swim the English Channel. It is also part of the 116-acre Kingsdown and Walmer Beach local nature reserve, which is attempting to preserve this vegetated coastal habitat and its associated fauna. Sea kale, sea pea and wild carrot can be found here. The latter is thought to

Bockhill Farm, another National Trust-owned stretch of coastline. (*Author's photograph*)

be responsible for the presence of a variety of moth species, including the Sussex Emerald, a breeding colony of which was confirmed here in 2010. Elsewhere along the 2 miles or so of beach toward Deal garden, escapees such as Red Hot Pokers and a number of non-native invasive plants have become established, threatening the indigenous wildlife.

The Blue Lady of Romney Codd

Kingsdown is another of those localities that seem steeped in legend. Here, this comes courtesy of local writer and former lightshipman George Goldsmith-Carter, who collected much of this lore over the years and recorded it in a very interesting, locally produced book entitled *Kingsdown and Ringwould: A History and Guide* (Ringwould is a small village a mile inland). Apparently, the countryside around and between these two villages has many traces of ancient habitation from at least the Mesolithic (Middle Stone Age) times. There are barrows, a ley line, and an old church with 1,000-year-old yew trees in the churchyard, and perhaps predictably there are many tales of ghostly encounters. A bend in the road as it passes through dark woodland near Ringwould, called Oxney Bottom, has a long tradition of a phantom 'grey lady' seen crossing the road, waving down a bus and, on one occasion, even getting on and then not being found, having supposedly disappeared. There are, of course, many such tales all over the country. Ringwould boasts several haunted houses and cottages, and there is talk of the tread of phantom footsteps on the footpaths and lanes around these villages.

The 'Moonraker Cliffs'. (*Author's photograph*)

A more unusual story, however, concerns the 'Blue Lady of Romney Codd'. This story was passed on to Mr Goldsmith-Carter by a Mrs Franks, an avid local folklore collector. Romney Codd was the name of an ancient village, now long gone, that once existed in a valley behind Kingsdown. The Blue Lady also takes part of her name from the colour she is said to display, variously said to be that of her gown or her ghostly luminosity. She is said to walk the cliff path above Oldstairs Bay, then pass through a fence, now in her way, to reappear with a slight moan on the path to the village street where she drinks from a well known as the 'blue well', a small spring on the track. A sighting of the Blue Lady is said to bring good luck, a good harvest, a good catch at sea, or more ominously a 'rich wreck', successful smuggling haul or death to an enemy. The last recorded sighting was apparently in 1860. What the origin and history of such a tale is I do not know, but it would certainly make an interesting project for some curious local folklorist to follow up.

The Goodwin Sands – 'The Ship Swallower'

Another nearby locality that has attracted much folklore is the 12-mile-long, 5-mile wide offshore sandbank known as the Goodwin Sands, which can be seen from the Kingsdown Cliffs at low tide. According to legend, they were once an island known as Lomea, or Low Island. It is said that back in the eleventh century, Earl Godwin (after whom the Sands are

View towards Walmer, Deal and the Isle of Thanet beyond and beach huts at Kingsdown. (*Photographs by Candida Wright*)

named) neglected to repair the sea defences of the island, which was subsequently inundated by the sea, so becoming the sandbank we see today. Modern scientific investigation shows that the sands lie on a bedrock of chalk, 78 feet below modern high-tide sea level. This proves that in historical times the Sands were only ever sands, never a solid island. A thousand years ago, if sea level was a little lower, they may perhaps have become uncovered more often and more extensively, so quite plausibly gaining the name 'Low Island'.

Legend apart, the Goodwins, nicknamed 'The Ship Swallower', have a fearsome history of shipwreck. It has been claimed that between 1,400 and 5,000 ships have foundered here, and over 50,000 mariners lost their lives here during historical times. The worst known wrecking incident was probably the infamous storm of November 1703, when hurricane-force winds forced many sailing vessels onto the Sands, with an estimated 1,500 seamen lost. Ships wrecked here often vanish from sight, as they are gradually engulfed by the shifting sands, sometimes to re-emerge years later for a while. If the Sands ever become joined to the mainland through silt accumulation and dry out, they will prove an irresistible magnet for any future archaeologist or treasure seeker. That, however, may be a project for the distant future.

Today, the Goodwin Sands are marked by three lightships and fifteen buoys. Even lightships, though, are vulnerable. On 28 November 1954, the South Goodwin Lightship was swept onto the Sands during a severe gale. All seven crew members were drowned but there was one survivor, Ronald Murton, an ornithologist who had been on the ship birdwatching.

On a lighter note, boat trips can be made to the Sands where there is now a substantial and growing colony of seals, some common but mostly grey, that can be seen at low tide. Occasionally, some brave souls play a cricket match here – rather them than me as the returning tide can quickly turn the ground underfoot to semi-liquid quicksand!

Ghost Ships of the Goodwin Sands

George Goldsmith-Carter in his various writings on local folklore has collected a number of tales of ships seen foundering in the vicinity of the Sands, which when investigated by would-be rescuers are not found. Later it was realised that the ship's description matches that of one lost on the Goodwins at some past date. Another ghost ship has been sighted!

Most of these tales relate to many years ago, and perhaps it was possible for a ship to be lost so quickly and completely that no trace was ever found.

Of interest to many, though, were the suggestions that the ghost ships reappeared on the anniversaries of their loss. The most well known of these legends was that of the *Lady Lovibond*. According to the story, this ship was wrecked on 13 February 1748, and was seen repeating its demise on the same date fifty years later in 1798 by a Captain James Westlake of the ship *Edenbridge*. On this date in 1848, fishermen on the shore reported a sailing vessel matching the description of the Lady Lovibond breaking up on the Sands. Fishing boats were hurriedly despatched but found no trace of the ship or any survivors of the supposed wreck. A similar incident is said to have occurred in 1898, so storytellers assured us that the spectral scene would replay again in 1948. That year, the 13 February was foggy and nothing was reported, so 1998 was eagerly awaited by the many thousands who had since read of the ghost ships in one of the many books on folklore and ghost stories that have appeared in recent decades.

So, on 13 February 1998, the foreshore at Deal, Walmer and Kingsdown was lined by hundreds of people hoping to catch a glimpse of, or perhaps film, this most famous of 'ghost ships'. Ghost hunters and television crews from all over Britain, as well as from France, Italy, Germany and America, descended on the area. People larked about, one group passing the end of Deal Pier in an inflatable boat, dressed as ghosts. Expectations were high but, of course, the *Lady Lovibond* failed to appear. This is not surprising really, since local historians of maritime history have not found any trace of a ship by this name having ever existed. Furthermore, Mark Frost of Dover Museum pointed out in 1998 that what had been 13 February in 1748 became 2 February after 1752 when England adopted the Gregorian calendar. Everyone was looking on the wrong day for a ship that never existed in the first place!

However, the *Lady Lovibond* is not the only claimed ghost ship of the Goodwin Sands. There is also the SS *Violet*. This was in fact a real ship, a cross-Channel steam packet that ran aground in a violent storm on 6 January 1857 and was lost with all hands. There is a gravestone in Dover's Cowgate Cemetery that records the loss of twenty-six-year-old Nathaniel Harmer with the SS *Violet* that night.

George Goldsmith-Carter hints in his 1953 book *The Goodwin Sands* that he and his fellow lightship crew may have seen a re-enactment of the grounding of the SS *Violet* on 1 January 1947. It was a similar ship that passed them in similarly bad weather, though not exactly the anniversary of course, being a few days out. This ship was lost to sight in fog as it headed for the Goodwins, though later Carter said they saw rockets 'pale and feeble' from the direction it went in. The Ramsgate lifeboat was called out but nothing was found, nor indeed any loss of a ship reported. But was this really the SS *Violet*, or another ship that reached its destination safely despite the fears of the lightship crew? Perhaps the 'pale and feeble' rockets seen were from some New Year festivities, either from this ship or some distant point on land. For the record, local fisherman 'Wimpey' Fishlock also claims to have seen the SS *Violet* on another occasion.

The End of the Cliffs

From the seafront at Kingsdown we get our last good view of the White Cliffs of Dover, beckoning the walker approaching from the north. As we continue past Kingsdown, the remainder of the cliffs gradually become more vegetated and much lower, eventually petering out next to Walmer Castle.

Walmer Castle

Walmer Castle was one of a series built in a concentric Tudor rose shape, as seen from above, on the orders of Henry VIII. They were all constructed between 1538 and 1540, and were intended to defend the country should the Pope have instructed the Roman Catholic powers to invade England in order to resolve outstanding differences with the King. The other castles in the series are at Camber in East Sussex, Sandgate, near Folkestone, Deal and Sandown (on the coast just north of Deal and now almost totally washed away by the sea). Walmer was no doubt a vulnerable point that needed to be guarded by a castle, being a flat shingle shore at the end of the cliffs. In fact, it is believed by many that Julius Caesar first made landfall in Britain on Walmer Beach back in 55 BC; a plaque on Walmer seafront commemorates the event.

As for Walmer Castle, it is best known today as the official residence of the Lord Warden of the Cinque Ports. The Cinque Ports are a confederation of five ports – Hastings, Romney, Hythe, Dover and Sandwich – with two associated ancient towns – Rye and Winchelsea – and a number of 'limbs', such as Folkestone, Deal, Kingsdown and Ramsgate, set up in the eleventh century to provide ships and men to help defend the coast and promote cross-Channel trade. The post of Lord Warden was created in the thirteenth century to help keep control over the organisation and establish a link to the crown. Initially, Lord Wardens

Kingsdown Beach and the end of the cliffs, or the beginning, depending on which way you are going of course. (*Author's photographs*)

Walmer Castle, official residence of the Lord Wardens of the Cinque Ports. (*Author's photograph*)

were based at Dover Castle, but were transferred to Walmer Castle in 1708. Some notable people have held this post, including the Duke of Wellington from 1829, Viscount Palmerston from 1861, and Sir Winston Churchill from 1941 – the best-remembered Lord Warden today of course being HRH Queen Elizabeth the Queen Mother, who held the post from 1979 until her death in 2002. The post is currently occupied by Admiral the Lord Boyce.

Today, Walmer Castle is managed by English Heritage and is open to the public. It has more the feel of a stately home than a military fortification, though there are still cannons pointing seaward. The castle has an elegant, eighteenth-century panelled interior, numerous relics and portraits of the Duke of Wellington and some fine gardens.

Leaving Walmer Castle and heading eastwards takes us across a flat, shingle landscape. Ahead lay the historic town of Deal with its maze of old smuggler's lanes and alleys. Beyond Deal is the Cinque Port of Sandwich, home to some 400 listed, medieval, Tudor and other historic buildings, and birthplace of such diverse inventions as the humble sandwich and Viagra. Further still brings us to the Isle of Thanet with its holiday resorts, Dickensian connections and Turner Gallery, but that is another journey for another time.

We have reached the end of our journey along the White Cliffs of Dover. It has not only been a geographical journey but also an historical one. From the laying down of the chalk,

The 'Moonraker Cliffs' from below. (*Author's photograph*)

the creation of the Channel and the cliffs, through the times of the earliest arrivals and settlers, the traders in bronze and iron, invaders from the Roman Empire followed later by Saxons, Normans, threats from Popes, from Spain, France, Germany and the Warsaw Pact, all have come and gone, and all have left their mark nowhere more than here on Britain's bulwark coast. There is another sort of history, too, a social and cultural history of events and tragedies, eccentric adventures, engineering achievements and contributions to science, literature, art and folklore, and we have seen plenty of evidence of all of that.

Of course it is not only human history but also natural history that is important here. The Kent Downs, the chalk cliffs, the offshore reefs, verdant undercliff and subtropical bays, all are precious environments and habitats. All contain a rich variety of flora and fauna of national importance. The concept of 'heritage' as something we inherit from the past and look after in the present to ensure its existence in the future applies to nature's creations too.

The White Cliffs of Dover are a special place, truly Britain's Heritage Coast. They are open for everyone to enjoy, to appreciate and to care for. I hope this book may not only help enhance that enjoyment and appreciation, but also encourage that care.

Chronology

80–64 million years ago	The Cretaceous Period: the chalk is laid down in a warm subtropical sea at the rate of 1 cm every 1,000 years.
c. 50 million years ago	The geological movements that cause the formation of the Alps also uplift the chalk beds creating the downlands of southern England.
6000 BC	Rising sea levels at the end of the last ice age lead to the formation of what we now call the English Channel, separating Britain from the European Continent. Subsequent erosion of the new coastline by rain and sea create the white cliffs that we see today.
1550 BC	A boat carrying a cargo of axes, daggers, chisels and other tools (some made of bronze) was wrecked under the cliffs at Langdon Bay, Dover. This is the oldest wreck of a seagoing vessel found anywhere in the world.
700 BC	'Quern' or milling stones made and exported from East Wear Bay near Folkestone. This trade continued until the end of the Roman period.
55 BC	Julius Caesar lands with a Roman expeditionary force on the beach at Walmer. He returns the following year. However, extended Roman occupation doesn't begin until 90 years later when the Emperor Claudius lands with a force of over 40,000 men at Richborough near the Isle of Thanet.
AD 100	Substantial Roman Villa in use at East Wear Bay. This site was occupied until around AD 390.
AD 180	Roman lighthouse (pharos) constructed on a hill above Dover to guide ships across the Channel from Boulogne.
AD 200	Hotel for traders and officials built in Dover. This has become known today as the Roman Painted House, on account of its fine examples of Roman mosaics and frescoes.
AD 280	Roman Painted House converted into a fort, in the face of instability within the Roman Empire and increasing Saxon raids.
Seventh Century	Early Christian church at present site of St Mary in Castro, Dover, in use.
1066	Normans build an earthwork castle at Dover.
1154–1187	Construction of much of the Dover Castle we see today, under Henry II.
1216/17	The siege of Dover Castle by barons supporting Prince Louis of France's bid for the throne of England. Hubert de Burgh successfuly holds the castle, despite the walls being breached, until the siege is lifted.
1538–40	Walmer Castle built along with a chain of other castles and defences on the orders of Henry VIII.
c. 1605	William Shakespeare produces *King Lear*, which features the cliffs near Dover, hence one of the cliffs to the west of the town becoming known as 'Shakespeare Cliff'.

1785	First ever flight across the Channel by balloonist Jean Pierre Blanchard.
1793	Revolutionary France declares war on Britain resulting in a substantial programme of new and upgraded coastal fortifications over the ensuing twenty years.
1805–12	A chain of seventy-four Martello towers are built along the coast between Folkestone in Kent and Seaford in Sussex as another line of defence against Napoleonic France. The feared invasion failed to materialise following Napoleon's defeat on the Continent and many of the towers were used as bases by a Preventative Force set up to combat smuggling along this coast.
1820	Following the arrest of some Folkestone smugglers and their internment in Dover Gaol, an angry mob from both Folkestone and Dover storm the gaol, tearing it down and releasing the prisoners. Soldiers sent to quell the disturbance refuse to fire on the crowd and the prisoners were never recaptured. An anonymous ballad was written about the event, which sometimes surfaces at local folk music fixtures.
1829	Duke of Wellington becomes Lord Warden of the Cinque Ports and officially resident at Walmer Castle.
26 January 1843	Round Down demolished near Shakespeare Cliff making way for the main line railway from London to Dover via Folkestone. In the process a large area of foreshore nicknamed the 'Great Fall' is created under the cliffs.
Summer 1843	First cross-Channel passenger ferry services begin from Folkestone to Boulogne.
c. 1833–60	Some local families inhabit caves beneath the cliffs near Dover. Depicted in contemporary paintings by W. H. Prior and Samuel Gillespie Prout.
1860	Charles Dickens in Dover.
1875	Matthew Webb becomes the first man to swim the English Channel.
1880	Folkestone headmaster H. Ullyett records his observations of wildlife in the Folkestone Warren in his publication *Rambles of a Naturalist Round Folkestone*.
1880	First attempt at digging a Channel Tunnel started on the site of the earlier mentioned 'Great Fall'. The project is abandoned the following year.
1883	Coal discovered on the site of the Channel Tunnel workings, near Shakespeare Cliff. The mine turns out a poor yield and closes in the early twentieth century.
24 December 1898	Marconi first demonstrates ship-to-shore radio at South Foreland lighthouse.
1899–1909	Construction of Admiralty Harbour. All trace of former cave dwellings swept away.
1909	Louis Bleriot becomes the first person to fly the Channel in a heavier than air aircraft, followed in 1910 by Charles Stewart Rolls, being the first to do it both ways in a single flight.
6 November 1910	Wreck of the SS *Preussen* beneath the cliffs at South Foreland.
1914–18	The First World War. Some seven million troops leave for the Continent from Folkestone Harbour over these years, many never to return.
1914	Nearly 65,000 Belgian refugees arrive at Folkestone Harbour having fled from German troops in their native country.

1915–1918	The Dover Patrol assembles a huge of vessels to defend the coast and keep the Channel seaways clear. A Royal Navy Airship Station operates from Capel-le-Ferne to help in the search for German U-boats. In 1918, the Dover Patrol carries out a daring raid on German forces based in Zeebrugge.
19 December 1915	Massive landslip at Folkestone Warren closes the mainline railway for three years. Troops help evacuate passengers from a stranded train en route to Dover. A large mock-Tudor house known as Eagle's Nest slides 100 feet down the cliff face. Its occupants, Fred and Emma Weston escape and take nearly six hours to cross the newly created tumbled terrain to reach a friend's house in Folkestone. The following year the house is dismantled and taken to a village near Ashford, where it is reassembled.
1921	Dover Patrol monument erected at St Margaret's Bay.
6 August 1926	Gertrude Ederle becomes the first woman to swim the English Channel, arriving at Kingsdown after swimming 35 miles in 14 hours 39 minutes.
1928	A sound mirror erected as a defensive measure on Abbot's Cliff. Sound mirrors were soon outdated by the development of radar. Today, they are all listed buildings and under the protection of English Heritage.
1939–45	The Second World War. This stretch of coast comes under intense and continuous bombardment from aircraft, shell fire from northern France, V1s and V2s. The area becomes known as 'Hellfire Corner'. The White Cliffs of Dover become known the world over as a result of Vera Lynn's song of that name.
1940	Operation Dynamo, the rescue of British and Allied troops from the beaches of Dunkirk by an armada of 'little ships', is masterminded from a control centre beneath Dover Castle by Vice Admiral Bertram Ramsay.
10 July–31 October 1940	The Battle of Britain rages in the sky above this part of Kent. The date 15 September is widely regarded as having been the decisive day of the Battle, after which Germany's Luftwaffe gradually accepted defeat.
1941	Winston Churchill becomes Lord Warden of the Cinque Ports.
1948–1953	British Rail undertakes major sea defence and cliff stabilisation works at Folkestone Warren, including the construction of two concrete aprons.
1952	Noel Coward sells his seaside home at St Margaret's Bay to Ian Fleming who later wrote the James Bond novels.
1954	Folkestone Warren reopened to the public after the area was cleared of mines and other Second World War defensive measures.
1955	Ian Fleming's third James Bond book *Moonraker* published. This was set largely on the coast between Dover and Deal.
1956	Little Switzerland campsite established at Folkestone Warren.
1959	First hovercraft crossing of the English Channel by an SRN1 arrives on beach at Dover Harbour.
1962	Dover Castle opened to the public. In the wake of the Cuban missile crisis, a Regional Seat of Government is established beneath the castle to operate in the aftermath of a nuclear attack. This remains in a state of readiness until its closure in 1984.
1965	Folkestone Warren camping/caravanning site established near the seashore.
1968	First substantial, commercial cross-Channel passenger hovercraft service begins between Dover and both Calais and Boulogne using the large, car-carrying SRN4 craft.
1970	Roman Painted House discovered in Dover town centre.
1972	Pines Garden opens at St Margaret's Bay.

1974	National Trust acquires Bockhill Farm, a substantial area of clifftop between St Margaret's Bay and Kingsdown. In subsequent years, more areas of adjacent land are purchased until almost the entire open coastline between Dover and Kingsdown is owned by the National Trust.
1977	The Jubilee Way flyover that takes road traffic directly up to the M2, bypassing the town, opens.
12 June 1979	Bryan Allen pedals the *Gossamer Albatross*, the first man-powered aircraft to cross the English Channel, from the apron at Folkestone Warren to Calais.
1979	HRH Queen Elizabeth the Queen Mother takes over as Lord Warden of the Cinque Ports from Sir Robert Menzies.
1987	Construction of the Channel Tunnel starts.
16 October 1987	Car ferry *Hengist* stranded on the apron at Folkestone Warren during the infamous hurricane.
1988	South Foreland Lighthouse made redundant.
1989	White Cliffs Countryside Project (now White Cliffs Countryside Partnership) formed, to manage the natural environment of the White Cliffs coastline and associated countryside.
1990	English Heritage open up to the public the formerly secret wartime tunnels beneath Dover Castle.
1993	Completion of the Channel Tunnel construction. It was officially opened on 6 May 1994.
10 July 1993	HRH Queen Elizabeth the Queen Mother opened the Battle of Britain Memorial at Capel-le-Ferne.
1994	Wreck of a Bronze Age boat discovered at Langdon Cliffs near Dover.
1997	Samphire Hoe, a nature reserve created by reclaiming land using spoil from the Channel Tunnel excavation on the site of the 1843 'Great Fall', opens to the public.
1 January 2000	First light of the new millennium strikes the South Foreland lighthouse at sunrise. This being where the sunrise is first seen in Britain on New Year's Day.
2000	National Trust Gateway Centre opens at Langdon Cliffs.
1 October 2000	Last SRN4 hovercraft flight across the Channel between Dover and Calais ends the era of large hovercraft being used as cross-Channel ferries.
January–February 2001	Major cliff falls at Folkestone Warren close footpaths and coincide with the disappearance of a local man.
2002	Admiral the Lord Boyce installed as new Lord Warden of the Cinque Ports, officially resident at Walmer Castle.
2002	Cross-Channel ferries cease to operate from Folkestone Harbour.
2008	Yves Rossy flies from Calais to a parachute landing near South Foreland lighthouse in just 13 minutes using a jetpack.
March 2012	Substantial cliff falls at South Foreland.
10 April 2012	First screening at the Quarterhouse in Folkestone of the film *Life's a Beach* about the life of Jeremy Francis (Mungo) on Abbot's Cliff beach.
August 2013	Cliff falls at Langdon Bay close footpath to the beach.
29 August 2013	National Trust publishes a list of top ten recommended walks in Britain. The White Cliffs of Dover are in the number one position.
9 September 2013	Wing Commander Bob Foster, one of the last of 'The Few', opens the construction phase of a new state of the art visitor centre called 'The Wing' at the Battle of Britain Memorial site at Capel-le-Ferne.

Bibliography

Burville, Peter and Julia, *The White Cliffs of Dover: Images of Cliff and Shore* (Triangle Publications, 2001; revised 2003)

Burville, Dr Peter, *An East Kent Family: The Burvilles* (self-published, 2005)

Foley, Michael, *Martello Towers* (Amberley Publishing, 2013)

'Felix', *Rambles Around Folkestone* (Glandfield, 1913)

Fleming, Ian, *Moonraker* (Pan, 1955)

George, Michael and Christine, *Dover & Folkestone during the Great War* (Pen and Sword [Military], 2008)

Harris, Paul, *Folkestone Warren in Old Picture Postcards* (European Library, 1993, 2001 and 2008)

Harris, Paul, *Ghosts of Shepway* (self-published, 1994; revised 1995 and 2000)

Harris, Paul, *Haunted Shepway* (Marlin Publications, 1998)

Hollands, Ray and Paul Harris. *Along the Kent Coast* (Sutton Publishing, 2003 and 2005)

Lane, Anthony, *Calamity Corner* (Tempus, 2004)

Lane, Anthony, *Front Line Harbour: A History of the Port of Dover* (Amberley Publishing, 2011)

Larn, Richard and Bridget, *Shipwrecks of the Goodwin Sands* (Meresborough Books, 1995)

Lees, Susan, *Capel-le-Ferne: The Village in the Clouds* (Capel-le-Ferne Parish Council, 2001)

Longden, Sean, *T Force: The Race for Nazi War Secrets, 1945* (Constable and Robinson, 2009)

Mackie, S. J., *Folkestone and its Neighbourhood with Gleanings from Municipal Records* (J. English, 1883)

Rankin, Nicholas, *Ian Fleming's Commandos: The Story of 30 Assault Unit in WWII* (Faber & Faber Ltd, 2011)

Soper, Tony, *A Natural History Guide to the Coast* (Peerage Books, 1984)

Tuson, Dan, *The White Cliffs of Dover & South Foreland Lighthouse* (National Trust, 2010)

Ullyett, H., *Rambles of a Naturalist Round Folkestone* (J. English, 1880)

Underwood, Peter, *Ghosts of Kent* (Meresborough Books, 1985)

Various, *Shakespeare Cliff: A People's History* (Dover District Council and White Cliffs Countryside Project, 2008)

Various, *Illustrated Guide to Britain's Coast* (Drive Publications, 1984; revised 1987)

Various, *Dover Castle* (English Heritage 1997; revised 2001)

Various, *Kingsdown and Ringwould: A History and Guide* (Wissant Society, 1989)

Wells, H. G., *Kipps: The Story of a Simple Soul* (Everyman/J. M. Dent, 1993, originally published in 1903)